Brian and Eileen Anderson

walk & eat
KEFALONIÁ

CONTENTS

2

If holidays are about new experiences, then this pocket guide will add a further dimension to your stay on Kefaloniá. It solves two problems — where to walk and where to find some good, traditional food. The gastronomical touch extends a little further, with recipes for some of the island's dishes, both specialities and traditional. There are strolls for hot days and longer walks to work up an appetite. If you're just after some recommendations for where to eat, look no further!

Highlights at a glance

- 10 day walks, each with topographical map
- 2 excursions — one a walking tour around Argostóli and the other to Itháca, the land of Odysseus
- recommended restaurants for the walks
- recipes to try out when self-catering or back home
- hints on wheat-, gluten- and dairy-free eating and cooking on the island

INTRO

THE WALKS

The walks in this book vary in length and difficulty. None is too strenuous and all can be done by a reasonably fit walker. The walks are spread around the island and there is at least one near every major resort. The island's bus service is good but limited, depending on where you choose to stay, but a hire car will give you best access to all the walks.

There isn't a great deal of walking information available for Kefaloniá and this book brings together 10 of the best walks.

THE EXCURSIONS

Argostóli, capital of the island, is built for pleasure. A broad promenade, fishermen selling their early-morning catch, the best fruit and veg market on the island, a shoppers' haven along the first stone-paved street on the island, aptly called Lithó-stroto and now pedestrianised, great eating places, the best museums and everything to make this excursion a great day out.

The second excursion travels by car ferry over a 'wine-dark sea' to the nearby mountainous island of Itháca. Check out the picturesque ports and sleepy villages and, for the romantics, places associated with Homer's hero, Odysseus, King of Itháca. Easily achieved on a day trip.

THE RESTAURANTS AND TAVERNAS

We have featured only restaurants where we have dined and which meet our guidelines. Obviously, an important tourist destination like Kefaloniá has many excellent restaurants catering for different tastes. We have not included those offering 'international cuisine' — dishes like peppered steaks and chicken Kiev, no matter how good they may be. Similarly, Chinese and Indian restaurants do not feature.

Our aim has been to find restaurants and tavernas serving good, traditional Greek food using fresh ingredients. Many restaurant owners are keen to advertise a 'Greek Cuisine' and yet you find only a tiny corner on the menu for traditional Greek dishes.

Restaurants and tavernas differ largely in presentation. In a restaurant you expect to find the table set with a table cloth and cutlery laid out ready, as you would in any restaurant. Proper wine glasses have recently made an appearance replacing the

Price guide

Restaurants and tavernas aren't graded or classified by the tourist authorities as they once were, and are no longer subject to price controls. In spite of this, the prices between the various establishments remain surprisingly similar. In general terms, it's much cheaper eating on Kefaloniá than at home.

The price guides in this book (€ to €€€) indicate 'very reasonable' to 'fairly pricey'. Remember that this guide relates not to prices at home, but to *prices on Kefaloniá* and is a comparison between the various tavernas and restaurants. The majority fall into the average category indicated by €€. Even so, it's always possible to enjoy a relatively inexpensive meal in a top restaurant by choosing carefully from the menu. There's usually a large choice of cheaper starter dishes which can easily make up a satisfying meal.

small tumblers which are still used in many tavernas. Expectations in a taverna are a little different. The table may have a plastic covering but little else. Shortly after sitting down, a paper table cloth will appear, be laid over the plastic and fixed with side clips. The cutlery arrives in the bread basket after your order has been placed. Other than presentation, there is little difference, the food may well be very similar in quality and price. Restaurants have grown out of tavernas and are only likely to be found in the larger towns.

Taverna sign

Even in the more expensive restaurants it's easy to enjoy a good meal by choosing carefully. The Greek menu offers so many starters, like the well-known Greek salad, taken together with *tzatzíki* and a jug of house wine, and you will certainly not need to raid the piggy bank to end up with a good light lunch.

Please be aware that no restaurant or taverna has paid in cash or in kind to be included in this guide.

THE RECIPES

Requests for recipes always brought a delighted and enthusiastic response. Then the difficulties started. Take a handful of this and a cup of that or take 12 eggs and so on. Weights and measures are quite foreign to them. One interesting aspect was drawing out of the chefs their preferred herbs. Traditional recipes passed down through the family use only local herbs which grow naturally or are grown commercially on the island. Chief of these is parsley, which is used in so many recipes as a flavouring or as decoration. Oregano and dill are commonly used, but spices feature far less often.

Many standard recipes can vary quite considerably. Kefalonian meat pie is a good example. Each one we tried and each recipe we acquired was different. Basically, it's a mix of meat and rice in a pie. Different size of meat cuts, different ratios of meat and rice, different herbs and spices were among the variations and, in one case, lentils replaced rice. Two tips from the Greeks when cooking dried beans. The first tip is, after soaking, bring to the boil, drain, and boil again in fresh water. This helps reduce flatulence. Secondly, to keep the skins tender, add the olive oil and salt five minutes before the end of cooking.

Acknowledgements

We would like to thank Dimitra Patrikios and Tassos Matsoukis of Ionian Island Holidays (www.ionianislandholidays.com) for providing us with superb accommodation in Fiskárdo. It is a delightful place to stay and gave us the opportunity to explore the region more thoroughly. Thanks also to Nick and Vivian Sklavounaki of Vivian Villa (www.kefalonia-vivianvilla.gr), our regular base in Argostóli, who have become good friends over the years as we researched our general guide to Kefalonia (published by Landmark). They have helped with our research on previous occasions, but this time Greek cooking was in the spotlight. Viv is a great cook, as we well know, so special thanks to her for tips and recipes. Also to Liana Sklavounaki for checking our Greek.

We owe our Fiskárdo walks to FNEC, Fiskárdo's Nautical & Environmental Club. Their young volunteers pioneered a number of walks in the area and cut a path for Walk 6 through a couple of kilometres of forest by hand! Thanks to them and, if you want to volunteer, check their web site: www.fnec.gr.

So we have drawn all our information together and tried to make the dishes at home to recapture the taste and flavour. It's difficult without exactly the same ingredients and, without the intangibles — the sunshine, the holiday atmosphere, the waves lapping on the sea shore — it's doubly difficult. Even so, the recipes are authentic and results pleasing.

Olive oil isn't good to use for frying at high temperatures, the lighter sunflower oil or similar is more commonly used by the Greeks for this purpose. If cooking at home, rape seed oil is as healthy as olive oil and better for frying. The Greeks tend to use olive oil excessively but the quantities have been reduced in our recipes.

EATING GREEK

Eating out for Greek families is a social occasion. It's a pleasure just to watch them. Family and friends gather around the table, men and women sometimes choosing to segregate themselves, with the children up and down as children are. When the food arrives, it's placed in the centre of the table for all to share. Plate after plate arrives until there's hardly room left. The chatter is long and loud, and the pace of eating is slow. Hot food cooling is of no concern. If it's a festive occasion, impromptu Greek dancing quite often follows.

Visitors, on the other hand, usually order a Greek salad for one person, perhaps a *tzatzíki* for another and so on. But there are so many different dishes and flavours to enjoy, it makes sense to **put all the starters in the middle and share**. If you indicate that you would like to eat this way, the waiter will

Selection of starters at Arkondikó in Argostóli: roasted aubergine salad, battered courgettes and, behind, *riganáda* (see page 44)

bring small empty plates for each person. Even with only two of you dining, two or three starters can be tried — but it's even better with four or more people eating. After the starters, it's much more acceptable to order individual main courses, although these can be treated in the same way as *mezédes* (appetizers) and shared. We became so used to sharing when living in Greece that we now often share starters and sweets — even in restaurants at home.

After decades of tourism, many tavernas now appreciate that you may not want every course you order to arrive at the same time. But some, especially in country areas, may *not* understand this, so it is best to order *mezédes* first, then order the rest later — or say *argótera* (later) for main courses, etc.

The Greeks **order certain dishes by weight**, usually lamb, pork chops or *kalamári* — all of which will be ordered by the kilo. A half kilo is usually plenty for two people and can be cheaper than ordering by the portion. Fish almost always appears on the menu priced by the kilo. It sometimes looks very expensive when you see the kilo price, but the fish will be weighed and a portion size is usually 300-400 g. If the fish you have chosen is particularly large, the waiter will weigh it for you and tell you its cost to get your agreement.

KEFALONIAN FOOD

Manéstra

Kefalonian food follows traditional Greek cuisine but not necessarily the full spectrum of dishes and there is one speciality not widely found elsewhere, Kefalonian meat pie. The island is famous for its *féta* cheese which is said to have originated on Kefaloniá. Strangely enough, there is no factory of any size on the island making it and production is left in the hands of the various villages. The result is that no two *fétas* taste the same!

Over the many years we've been travelling to Greece and enjoying Greek food, the cuisine has always remained traditional and constant but there are now signs of change. Cooking programmes on Greek television are bringing a more progressive influence to the cuisine, and traditional dishes are starting to evolve. At the moment this is most noticeable in the salads which are improving in variety and content. Balsamic vinegar, an influence from its close connection with Italy, is a recent introduction on Kefaloniá.

One quick and easy hot one-pan meal we *do* make in self-catering (and often at home) uses a rice-like pasta, *manéstra*. On Kefaloniá, this is also known by its Italian name, *orzo*. Look for it in the pasta section on supermarket shelves. It looks just like rice and comes in three sizes, small *(mikró)*, medium *(métrio)* and large *(megálo)*. Greek friends recommend the medium size for general use. Look for *kritharáki métrio* or the Italian *orzo medio,* both names under the *manéstra* umbrella. If you make this at home, however, you'll have to bring packets of pasta home from Greece unless you live near a Greek produce supplier or specialist delicatessen. Below is our basic 'throw together' recipe; experiment with it and come up with your own variations. We prefer *manéstra* to rice, as it absorbs flavours beautifully and is so easy to use. But, naturally, if you need a gluten-free option, it's a good recipe for a *risotto.*

Using 50-75 g of pasta per person, select some pre-cooked diced meats (chicken, turkey, pork, etc) and vegetables suitable for a stir fry (chopped onion, garlic, peppers, courgettes, celery, broccoli florets, frozen peas … whatever). Heat olive oil or sunflower oil in a large frying pan/wok, and gently stir fry the *fresh* vegetables with the pasta briefly. Then dissolve a stock cube or two in 250 ml water and stir into the pan. Add more water if necessary. Cover and simmer for 6 min. Stir and check the water, then add seasoning, herbs, the meat and the *frozen* peas (if used). Cover, bring back to a simmer, and cook a further 5 min. The pasta should be soft if the dish is ready and the moisture absorbed. Serve on its own or with crusty bread and green salad.

THE MENU

Menus *(katálogos)* are becoming more helpful thanks to a recent directive. Restaurants have been asked to give some indication of the contents of a dish and to indicate dishes that contain ingredients cooked from frozen. The latter is done usually by adding an asterisk or the word *katef*, short for *katepsegménos*.

Life would be simpler if the menu in Greece was always set out in the familiar way of starters, main courses and sweets. It sometimes is, but then often further divided or subdivided. Fortunately, menus are usually available in English — although they are not always as helpful as they might be. A number of dishes have no direct equivalent. *Hórta (xórta),* for example, is a dish variously described as boiled greens or spinach. It's the green leaves of the dandelion family (but not strictly dandelions), sometimes collected wild, which are boiled, strained, seasoned, amply tossed in olive oil and lemon juice and served as a single vegetable dish. On Kefaloniá there is a similar dish, called *tsigaridiá.* Very good if it's fresh — a great favourite with the Greeks, and one of our favourites too. Similarly, familiar dishes such as *mousakás* are described in all sorts of ways — 'meat pie with béchamel sauce' is fairly typical.

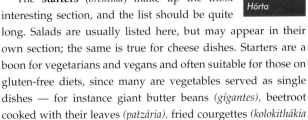

Hórta

The **starters** (*orektiká*) make up the most interesting section, and the list should be quite long. Salads are usually listed here, but may appear in their own section; the same is true for cheese dishes. Starters are a boon for vegetarians and vegans and often suitable for those on gluten-free diets, since many are vegetables served as single dishes — for instance giant butter beans (*gígantes*), beetroot cooked with their leaves (*patzária*), fried courgettes (*kolokithákia*

13

Boiled vegetables (above) and tzatzíki at Koros (page 68)

tiganitá), fried aubergines *(melitzana tiganitá)* and the already-mentioned *hórta*. Boiled vegetables (usually courgettes and green beans) may not sound appealing, but can be beautifully presented and delicious with lemon and olive oil or a dip.

There's an interesting array of **dips** — from the familiar *taramasaláta* (cod's roe) and *tzatzíki* (yoghurt/cucumber/garlic) to aubergine dip *(melitzanosaláta)* and garlic/mashed potato *(skordaliá or aliátha)*. On Kefaloniá *skordaliá* is often served to complement other dishes, particularly cod fish. These dips sometimes appear under the salad list.

Surprisingly, **soups** are a common feature on Kefalonian menus — usually bean, lentil, meat and vegetable. Another Kefalonian special, often seen on the menu as 'mushed eggs', is *strapetsáda*. This is scrambled **eggs** in spicy sauce with *féta* cheese.

Cheese *(tirí)* dishes on the starters list include *féta* sprinkled with herbs and drizzled with olive oil, *saganáki* (fried *féta* — or another cheese), *saganáki sto foúrno* (oven-baked *féta* with tomatoes and peppers, often spicy), grilled *haloúmi* (a dish borrowed from Cyprus), *tirosaláta* (a spicy cheese dip), and *tirokeftédes* (cheese croquettes).

Greek **salad** *(horiátiki saláta)* is synonymous with Greek cuisine for most visitors. There is no standard; it depends on the season, but tomato, cucumber and olives are ever-present, topped by a lump of *féta* cheese and often liberally soaked in olive oil and vinegar. Sometimes it can be a meal in itself. It's on every menu and serves as a useful price comparison between tavernas. Very often we prefer just to have a salad of tomato and cucumber *(domáta/angoúri)*. One salad mostly ignored by visitors, but popular with the Greeks, is lettuce salad *(maroúli saláta)*. It doesn't sound very exciting, but is really tasty the way it's prepared. Salads are slowly evolving, cherry tomatoes replacing or supplementing the large Mediterranean tomato, rocket leaves and roasted aubergine adding much more variety.

The **main courses** are listed under *entrádes*, grills and/or meat *(kréas)*, or there may be just one list. Normally, under the *entrádes* you can expect to find **Greek specialities** like *mousakás*, *stifádo* (a veal and shallot stew), *kokkinistó* (veal stew with tomatoes) and *giouvétsi* (veal in a clay pot with *manéstra*, the rice-like pasta mentioned on page 11); the **grills** are found in other sections. **Fish** *(psári)* or **seafood** *(thalasiná)* are normally listed separately.

Beef is served in the form of veal *(moskári)* — beef from a milk-weaned yearling animal. Steaks seem to appear on restaurant menus, whereas tavernas stick with chops *(brizóla)* which are large and meaty. Pork chops *(hoiriní brizóla)* and lamb cutlets *(païdákia)* are popular, but these meats are also served on skewers as *souvláki*. Chicken and fish are also sometimes served this way. Goat *(katsíki)* is popular on Kefaloniá, and is eaten as chops or a roast which, like lamb, can be ordered by the kilo or by the portion *(merída)*.

Poultry is almost invariably chicken *(kotópoulo)*, but turkey *(galópoula)* is found occasionally.

On a visit to a good supermarket or a market, you will see fresh vegetables in abundance, but you are unlikely to see many **vegetables** with your main course — if any. Chips are fairly ubiquitous, but some dishes like squid *(kalamári)* are served without, so you may need to enquire. Chips *(patátes tiganités)* are always available as a side order with your starters or main course. If you just ask for *patátes,* it's generally understood you want *chips.* In one or two tavernas on Kefaloniá, particularly in Argostóli, there is often a choice of potato — from chips to boiled or jacket.

It's fairly typical to find **fish restaurants around coastal regions**. Although predominantly serving fish, fish restaurants invariably offer a selection of meat dishes. *Kalamári* is always popular, especially with the Greeks. Fresh is always best, tastier and more succulent, but not always available. Frozen can be good but more variable in quality. Octopus *(xtapódi)* is usually offered as grilled or cooked in wine or vinegar. Swordfish *(ksifías)*, salmon *(solómos)*, salt cod *(bakaliáros)*, and shrimps *(garídes)* are regulars on the menu. Of the smaller fish, *maridáki* and *atheriná* reach the menu in September, sardines *(sardéles)* and *gavros* are summer season dishes. *Gavros* is translated as anchovy, but they are most definitely *not* anchovies.

Desserts are listed under *glyká,* which means 'sweet'. The Greeks have a sweet tooth and love their sweets soaked in syrup and honey. But these sweets are not a major feature of taverna menus and sometimes don't appear at all. Very often the taverna owner will bring complementary fresh fruit, depending on the season. It might be grapes, watermelon or oranges, but one of our favourites is sliced apple dusted with cinnamon and drizzled with honey. Restaurants usually offer a better menu for desserts.

One of the most popular sweets with tourists is yoghurt and honey which may be topped with walnuts. It's not really a traditional Greek sweet, but a response to its immense popularity with visitors. Even if not on the menu, it can often be rustled up for you, since the taverna is likely to have a stock of thick, strained yoghurt for making *tzatzíki*.

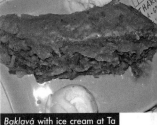

Baklavá, *kataïfi* and *halvá* are amongst the intensely sweet sweets. *Baklavá*, multi-layered filo pastry

Baklavá with ice cream at Ta Pitharia in Skála (page 134)

sandwiching finely chopped almonds or walnuts, rich in butter and soaked in sugar/honey syrup, finds many devotees (125 g = 695 calories). *Kataïfi*, best described as small shredded wheats (actually a pastry), soaked in sugar/honey syrup appeals to the same group of supporters, as does the *halvá*, a brown, sugar-rich sesame seed confection which is poured into a mould to set. *Galaktoboúriko* comes in much lower down the calorie scale. It's vanilla custard sandwiched between layers of filo pastry. *Loukoumádes*, batter balls soaked in honey syrup, is another sweet.

17

Frappé

In the heat of summer this is a popular drink for Greeks as well as tourists. Easy to make yourself, either in one of the cheap plastic *frappé* shakers (available in supermarkets) or in a jar with a screw cap. For each *frappé*, put a teaspoon of instant coffee in the container, add ice cubes then half water and half milk (fresh milk, the Greek evaporated milk called *Noynoy*, or soya), plus sugar if wanted. Shake vigorously until the coffee has dissolved and it's nice and frothy.

Coffee *(kafé)* deserves a special mention. At one time, only 'Nes' (short for Nescafé or any instant coffee) was available: strong enough to 'stand up' the proverbial spoon, it was served with a glass of water. Nowadays, water is still often served, but other options such as filter and cappuccino are commonplace. *A word of caution:* Greek Nes (Nescafé) is stronger and more bitter than its UK equivalent, so use it sparingly when you buy it for use at your hotel or in self-catering.

If you do happen to be in an establishment which only serves Nes, and you're not a lover of very strong coffee, ask for it *elafrí*, weak. Another pitfall to watch out for is added sugar. The Greeks normally have sugar in their coffee, which is some-times added automatically when it's made. As well as *elafrí*, you need to add *horís zákari* (without sugar). You may require your coffee with/without milk *(me/horís gála)*.

Ordering a **Greek coffee** is quite different. Sugar is added during the preparation, so you need to specify *glykó* (sweet), *métrio* (medium) or *skéto* (without sugar). Greek coffee is never served with milk.

Tea *(tsái)* is widely available — even herbal teas — in restaurants and some cafés. But in some older establishments and in country areas, where tea drinkers are more of a rarity, the need for boiling water to make a decent 'cuppa' hasn't quite filtered through. Don't be surprised if your tea arrives lukewarm. *Zestó vrásto neró* (boiling water) and bubbling gestures with your hands might help!

KEFALONIAN WINES

Vines are grown extensively on Kefaloniá, especially in the Omalá Valley, around St Gerasímos Monastery, and there are a good number of wine producers on the island. The most important grape variety is the *robola*, a Kefalonian speciality, which produces a refreshing, medium-bodied white wine with hints of citrus. This is sold in the shops as Robola from Cephalonia. Other grapes for white wine include *tsaoussi*, *zakyntho*, *vosilidi* and muscat. Red wines are generally not of the same quality, and the most

Be sure to visit the Robola Winery when you're near Valsamáta (Walk 3).

commonly used grape here is *mavrodaphne*. One of the best reds we found is sold as Linos.

In spite of the best efforts of the wine producers to promote the leading labels, the bulk wine released for sale as house wine is virtually the same standard. It's so good and so much cheaper that everybody drinks it, and we have yet to have a house wine, especially white, on Kefaloniá that disappointed us. We rated one house wine, made at Taverna Koros in Valsamáta, superior to any we tasted in bottles, and, of course, at a fraction of the price. It's so popular the customers buy it to take away.

House wines are bought by the kilo, which is effectively the same as a litre. It's a hangover from the days when you went along to the shop with your jug to buy wine from the barrel. For four people your first order would be a kilo, but two might start with a half-kilo (*misó kilo*) and take it from there.

RETSINA, OÚZO — AND BEER

It's said that resinated wine, or retsína, originated in the days before wine bottles, when wine was stored in jars or skins sealed with pine resin. When bottles came on the scene, the wine without the resin flavour was not universally popular, so retsína was born. It's generally much preferred by the Greeks — but less so on Kefaloniá, possibly because the quality of the house wines is so good. Provided the wine is only lightly resinated, it can be quite palatable, and the resin stabilises the wine — which gives it consistency. Our favourite is Malamátina. Kourtáki is the best-known brand internationally, but this is moderately resinated and not the easiest retsína for the uninitiated to fall in love with at first sip! Often a pale-coloured retsína signifies less resin, making a more palatable drink for first-timers.

Oúzo is a drink for bright sunshine and bonding, Greek-style. This aniseed-flavoured drink is taken with ice and water and, traditionally, a few nibbles. There are still one or two *oúzeri* around, where you can sit with an oúzo and expect some free *mezédes* (*mezés* for short) — a little plate with a piece of cheese perhaps, a chunk of bread, maybe a few cold chips, or anything to hand. But this tradition is now only usual in country villages away from mass tourism.

When we lived on Lesvos some years ago, the locals insisted that Lesvos made the best oúzo in Greece. We put this down to local pride, but since then we have travelled to many other Greek islands and, sure enough, everybody tells us the best oúzo is from Lesvos. Oúzo 12, Mini and Barbayanni are all leading brands.

One or two international **beers** are available, but Mythos and Amstel, lager-type beers, are freely available, both bottled and draught, and suit the sunny hot weather well.

PLANNING YOUR VISIT
When to go

Although one or two hotels in Argostóli remain open all year, Kefaloniá is effectively closed for tourism in winter. Lids come off the paint tins in April, when work starts and the island comes to life to get ready for the new season. This is about the earliest time that can be considered, although getting there will mean taking an international flight to Athens and an internal flight to Kefaloniá, often called Kafaliniá on airport departure boards — a journey which can usually be achieved in one day. Direct charter flights start in May and continue well into October.

The best time for walkers is in the **spring and autumn** months. Late April/May is a great time to be there walking. The temperature isn't too high, and the spring flowers are a definite bonus. The heat starts to build quickly in June, and at some point it becomes too hot to enjoy strenuous walks — but some of the easy or short walks remain possible, especially with an early start. July, August and early September are generally too hot for walkers unless you are prepared to rise with the sun and walk very, very early in the morning. Walking in the full heat of the sun in this period is risking serious heat exhaustion and is *most definitely not recommended.* Temperatures decline slowly throughout September, and usually by the middle of the month, walking is back on the agenda — but it may still be advisable to avoid strenuous walks for a time. By October the temperatures are usually back to the mid or low 20s and walking becomes a pleasure again.

But eating is a pleasure to be enjoyed any time of the year so, even if it's too hot to walk, you might still want to try some of our suggested restaurants and tavernas!

Where to stay

Our preferred base is **Argostóli** simply because it lies at the hub of the island and is well served by public transport. It has no beach, which will not please a lot of people, but it's not far from Lássi and a number of beaches. Argostóli has the only sizeable fruit and vegetable market on the island, and the town offers some of the best eating, although not everywhere is good.

Moving around the island counter-clockwise from Argostóli:

Lássi, very much a ribbon development along the main road, has a selection of good beaches and is a popular resort. It also has the advantage of being very close to Argostóli, close enough to walk the short main road route (2km) or the longer old carriageway route which is one of our featured walks.

Lourdáta: features in many brochures and has a good beach, but is a very quiet, isolated resort; a hire car will be essential to see anything of the island, since there is a limited bus service.

Kateliós: another small resort with plenty of character; it is also isolated, but at least lies on the bus route.

Skála: has developed into the island's leading resort, but is still not large. A huge sandy beach with plenty of space, a wide choice of tavernas and restaurants, good shopping and a walk on the doorstep.

Póros: lots of scenic character being nudged into the sea by the mountains, but losing out to neighbouring Skála in development. It remains popular, particularly with those who prefer its fine shingle beach and enjoy its huge promenade. There are plenty of places to eat, and more in the adjacent port which we feature for our two Póros walks. Ferries ply back and forth from this port to Killíni (a good connection for ferries to Zákynthos) and Pátras, both on the Peloponnese mainland.

Sámi: another major ferry port with a wide sea-front captured by tavernas and restaurants. Much of the accommodation lies back from the town, sometimes a fair distance. Its beach lies on the Karavómilos side or, if you are prepared to walk (3.5km) or take a taxi, you can visit the stunning white shingle beach of Antísamos. We feature a good footpath walk up to ancient Sámi from here.

Ag Efimía: an attractive but low-key fishing village and

House in Ássos

yachting centre. It has no beach to write home about. Some walking information is displayed on a board in the harbour to help you across the neck of the island to Mírtos beach on the other coast. Not all, but much of this walk is along the main road.

Fiskárdo: this delightful yachting harbour enclosed by pastel-coloured houses is a gem of a place to visit. Endless restaurants and tavernas spread around the quayside keep the place buzzing by day and lend a charming atmosphere to the evening. As a place to stay it's rather small, with a tiny town beach and a larger, shingle beach not too far away. We feature a fairly lengthy walk from here which can be used just to reach the shingle beach at Émblissi and visit on an excursion.

Ássos: another place of charm and character visited on one of our walks. It lies on the neck of a peninsula overlooked by a Venetian castle.

What to take

There is no special dress code for dining, except that shorts are not always appreciated in restaurants and some tavernas during the evening.

It's more important to concentrate on packing suitable walking gear. Walking boots are the footwear we most strongly recommend, but not all the walks demand them. Some of the track walks are fairly easy underfoot, and for these we prefer **walking shoes** or specialist walking trainers, especially if the weather is hot. Each person should carry a **small rucksack** and it's advisable to pack it with a **sunhat**, **suncream**, **first-aid kit** and some extra **warm clothing**. A **long-sleeved shirt** and **long trousers** should be worn or carried for sun protection and for walking through spiny vegetation. You should always carry a **mobile phone**; the **emergency number** on Kefaloniá (as throughout the EU) is 112.

Depending on the season, you may also need lightweight **rainwear** and a lightweight folding **umbrella** (which can also be useful for sun protection on sun-exposed sections of a walk). Some of our walks end up at a beach, so **swimwear** could be usefully included. A reliable litre-size **water bottle** is well worth packing, although small, easily carried bottles of water can be bought all over the island. *It is imperative that each walker carries at least a half-litre of water — a full litre or more when the weather is hot.*

Planning your walks

Look over the walks you plan to take in advance, to check out **transport**. There may be a walk or two on your doorstep and, depending where you stay, one or two more may be reached by public transport but the remainder will require a hire car or taxi.

We have **graded** the walks with the weekend walker in

mind, based on an ambient temperature *below the mid 20s C.* When temperatures rise above this level, walkers expend more energy simply keeping cool, and uphill walking especially is much more tiring. The **walking times** given at certain points always refer to the total walking time from the start and are based on an average rate of 4km per hour and allowing an extra 15min for every 100m/330ft of ascent. These time checks are not intended to predetermine your own pace, but are meant to be useful reference points. A walk might easily take you *twice as long* if you dawdle over the scenery, nature-watch or stop for the thousand little reasons which bring walkers to a halt.

Our walking **maps** are based in part on the Road Editions map mentioned on page 27, updated by our notes in the field. We have enlarged our maps to a scale of 1:50,000 to include a bit more detail, but the only paths shown on our maps are those we *know* to be viable.

Walking safely depends in great part on *knowing what to expect and being properly equipped.* For this reason we urge you to read through the *whole* walk description at your leisure *before* setting out, so that you have a mental picture of each stage of the route and the landmarks. One or two of these walks are waymarked, but **waymarks** may be found along parts of the others. *Only follow waymarks if they are confirmed by the route description.*

Thunderstorms in late autumn, after a long summer drought, can cause **flash flooding**, potentially a serious danger to walkers. Keep an eye on the forecast at this time of the year and do not take risks with the weather.

ON ARRIVAL
Tourist information

Not all resorts have a Tourist Information Office, but one can be found in Argostóli, Sámi and Póros. There are some walk leaflets available for Póros and Sámi. These leaflets are good on historical background but poor on route directions. In any case, the walks are described in this book.

Bus timetables are usually available at the tourist offices, but see under 'Transport' below.

The best **map** of the island is the 1:70,000 Road Editions map No. 304, which can be bought on the island or at home before you go.

Transport

KTEL provide a reliable bus service between Argostóli and Skála, Póros, Kateliós, Fiskárdo, Ag Efimía and Sámi. Unfortunately, the service is limited to only about two buses a day in each direction, except for Ag Efimía which has just one bus per day.

Outside Argostóli, there *are* other services, for example between Ag Efimía and Sámi. The full bus timetable can be checked on-line at www.kefalonia.net.gr/en/infoID.asp? Entityid=83, and timetables are available in bus stations and tourist offices. Bus fares are very inexpensive.

Taxis are widely available in Argostóli and most other tourist centres. When three or four people are sharing, they can be reasonably cheap and a more convenient option than the bus. Most taxi drivers on Kefaloniá speak English, so you should be able to establish the fare before setting out or make sure the journey is being metered.

Shopping for self-catering

Most self-catering accommodation on Kefaloniá is limited to facilities for throwing breakfast together. There are usually two hot plates combined with a fridge unit, and cooking utensils are minimal. There was a time — very recently — when we calculated that it was better value to eat out than buy food to cook yourself. It may not hold true now, but it's not so much more expensive to dine out in a taverna.

Few people want to waste warm evenings cooking when they could be out enjoying the atmosphere. There are one or two meals which can be assembled quickly without toiling in the heat. Salads are easy enough to put together, and most supermarkets have a **vegetable** section of some kind. Larger supermarkets offer a better choice of fresh vegetables — as do the local outdoor

Supermarket shopping list
washing-up liquid
washing powder for hand washing (look for the hand wash logo on the box and the word *xépi,* the Greek word for 'hand')
olive oil soap (excellent for removing stubborn stains when hand washing)
soap
paper towels and/or napkins
aluminium foil
tissues/toilet paper
scouring pads
salt & pepper
herbs & spices
mineral water
milk
coffee/tea/drinking chocolate
butter
sugar
bread
juice
wine/beer/oúzo
sunflower oil (cooking)
olive oil (salads) & vinegar
eggs
tomato purée
rice/pasta
mayonnaise/mustard/sauces

markets. Lettuce, tomatoes, onions, cucumbers and peppers are basics which most supermarkets stock. Remember these are often **local produce** and are *not treated or sprayed* in any way to make them look or stay fresh, so they may look a little sad towards the end of the day.

Freshly barbecued chicken is also available daily and always a good start for a basic meal. Some of the dips, like *tzatzíki* and *taramasaláta,* can be bought ready-made but, to make your own *tzatzíki,* head for the **delicatessen** counter and buy the strained yoghurt *(filtráro yiaoúrti)* found in a large white plastic drum. Ask for it by weight: we find a half kilo *(misó kiló)* more than enough for two, and it's packed in a plastic container for you. This is the really thick strained yoghurt used by the tavernas to make their own *tzatzíki,* and it is also ideal for yoghurt and honey. (When making any of our recipes back home, Total yoghurt, made in Greece, is the one to use.)

The delicatessen counter is where you can buy your **cheese**, too, and there is a much larger selection than just *féta.* Avoid *féta* which has been left on display and allowed to dry out. It loses texture and becomes strongly flavoured. Always buy your *féta* from the drum where it has been kept moist under brine. There are a number of hard cheeses to choose from, including *kefalo-tíri,* well worth trying, and *kaserí.* Soft cheeses are *féta* (also available from Total in the UK) and *myzíthra.* Greeks love their *myzíthra,* a low-fat cheese rather like a smooth cottage cheese. If you can buy it unsalted (often available in spring), it's great with honey for breakfast; the rest of the year it's usually salted.

Vegetarians, vegans and those on **dairy-free** diets should have no problem finding suitable food, but **gluten-free** products are much harder to find. Gluten intolerance as a dietary problem is little recognised and rarely diagnosed on Kefaloniá. We didn't find much evidence of ready-made gluten-free products apart from rice cakes in large supermarkets, and at the time of writing there were no health food shops.

Meat and **fish** can be bought from the big supermarkets. Except for octopus, squid, tuna and swordfish steaks, most species of fish on sale may be unfamiliar. In spring and autumn, small fish like whitebait are available, which can be dipped in flour, fried and eaten whole.

> ## Vegetarian, vegan, dairy- and gluten-free recipes
>
> The two books listed below contain straightforward recipes for those with special dietary needs. Both are worth considering if you plan to self-cater in Greece, and both are lightweight paperbacks easily packed in your luggage. They are available from www.amazon.co.uk
>
> **Greek Vegetarian Cooking** by Alkmini Chaitow is a book with plenty of excellent recipes and menu suggestions. It also indicates which recipes are dairy- and/or gluten-free.
>
> **A Vegan Taste of Greece** by Linda Majzlik offers plenty of recipes to sample, and a concise, comprehensive listing and description of ingredients. Equally useful for vegetarians and for those on dairy- or gluten-free diets.

Ready-cleaned fish from the freezer offers an easier option for self-catering. Small, ready-made-up *souvláki* (**meat on a spit**) can usually be bought from the meat counter or butchers — handy if you are staying in a complex with a communal barbecue. Similarly, the **sausage** on Kefaloniá is packed with meat and another great favourite for the barbecue. All the usual selection of chops and chicken pieces is on offer.

Fruit & veg market

Argostóli has the only large fruit and vegetable market on the island, and it's open six days a week. It's located on the harbourside and does brisk business, especially in the morning.

Just about everything can be bought here, from fruit and vegetables to olives and honey.

Fruit & veg market, Argostóli

Some of the vegetables may be unfamiliar, especially the greens, but they are generally named. By the way, don't expect the celery to be well blanched, it generally isn't, and there is another, unfamiliar form of celery, *célino,* which is much smaller. If you want to try your hand at cooking *hórta,* then you can buy the cultivated leaves here.

There is no fish market, but fish can be bought directly from the fishermen at the quayside in the mornings and in the supermarkets.

Argostóli, capital of the prefecture of Kefaloniá and Itháca (Itháki), spreads along the east-facing shore of an inland gulf. This circular walk around the town takes in all the major points of interest. Morning is the best time to visit; it quietens down in the afternoon, when some shops close.

argostóli

EXCURSION

Back in the 16th century Argostóli was no more than a scattering of fishermen's cottages. Building a port in this sheltered bay brought a steady increase in shipping trade and in the town's development. By 1753 it had become such an important trading centre that it was petitioning its governors in Venice to become adminis- trative capital. In 1759, St George's Castle (see page 39) relinquished its role, and Argostóli was made capital.

It developed into a graceful town with elegant Venetian-style mansions and bell towers. Early in the 19th century it came under British administration, and the first governor was the Swiss Phillipe de Bosset (1810-14), a colonel in the British Army. He brought about improvements in the island's infrastructure, including building the Drápano Bridge (see page 35) and the road over to Sámi. Colonel Sir Charles Napier, appointed governor in 1821, was just as keen to see further improvements, and more roads and public buildings followed. He created the first public park in Argostóli, Napier Gardens, which remains today, inland from the main square.

See plan inside the front cover

Grade/time: easy; allow half a day or more

Transport: 🚌 or 🚗 to Argostóli. If you arrive by bus, walk north along the front from the southern end and join the walk at the fruit and veg market. Arriving by car, the northern end of town, just beyond the Lixoúri ferry, offers the best chance of finding a parking spot on the front.

Refreshments: cafés, fast-food outlets, tavernas and restaurants; see our suggestions on pages 40-41.

Opening times
Archaeological Museum: Tue-Sun from 08.30-15.00
Folklore Museum: Mon-Sat from 09.00-14.00

Elegance and culture ensured a good standard of living right through until the World Wars of the 20th century and the Greek Civil War which followed, when life was seriously disrupted. Just as a settled existence was returning, the 1953 earthquake (see pages 66-67) brought utter and complete devastation to the island — persuading many thousands to emigrate. Rebuilding was slow and difficult for a time but, with the help of money being sent home, grander buildings started to appear in Argostóli. Venetian-style architecture still influences present-day Argostóli, and with a large music school and theatre, its cultural aspirations remain undimmed.

Start the walk by strolling along the promenade past the **Lixoúri ferry terminal** (1). (One of our featured tavernas, **Patsoúras** (2), lies across the road from the Lixoúri ferry, near or a little north of where you might park.) Taking the ferry over to Lixoúri is another trip to try sometime. The fare is extremely low for foot passengers, the journey time around 25 minutes, and the ferries run every 30 minutes in high season and hourly at other times. The ferry docks right in Lixoúri town, so no other transport is needed, and you can be seated at a shaded café table in the impressive main square within minutes. Alternatively, you could try Walk 2.

For now continue along the front, very shortly passing the **Greek National Tourist Office** (3). Recently modernised, it has some walk leaflets. Palm trees line the now-wide promenade as the **fishing boat area** (4) is approached. This is the place to buy your fresh fish, straight off the boat. This activity always gathers interested spectators — especially the friendly logger-

Drápano Bridge

Early in the 19th century, the first governor under British administration, Philippe de Bosset, a Swiss Colonel in the British Army,

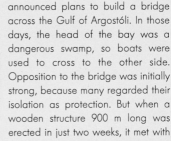

announced plans to build a bridge
across the Gulf of Argostóli. In those
days, the head of the bay was a
dangerous swamp, so boats were
used to cross to the other side.
Opposition to the bridge was initially
strong, because many regarded their
isolation as protection. But when a
wooden structure 900 m long was
erected in just two weeks, it met with
instant approval. It was eventually replaced by a stone
bridge which, amazingly, was one of only a few structures
to survive the earthquake. The obelisk dedicated to de
Bosset part-way across gives a construction date of 1813.

With the steady increase in traffic, the bridge was
threatened with closure for a number of years. Finally, in
2005, it was closed to traffic, but remains open to
pedestrians. There is a clamour to have it reopened to
traffic, but whether the necessary rebuilding will ever
take place remains in doubt.

The bridge now makes an excellent, if short, walk across the bay,
with the sea on one side and the lagoon which the bridge creates
on the other. On reaching the far side from Argostóli, keep ahead
along the road for a few minutes, to reach the walled British
cemetery on the right. The iron gates easily push open, and a notice
board inside lists all the known graves going back almost two
centuries. Almost 200 British soldiers and their families are buried
here.

head turtles. The low bridge you can see crossing the gulf is **Drápano Bridge** (see previous page).

Further along are the **fruit and veg, meat and fish markets** (6), with plenty of fresh produce on view. Most of the stalls are on the seafront side, but there are one or two opposite. Look for *hórta* among the green, leafy vegetables which are usually labelled; it's delicious and quite common on taverna menus (see page 13). Local traders have stalls at the end of this market but they also have their own small market area behind the **bus station** (7), just a little further out. On reaching the Shell petrol station, look inland from the Shell sign to find Vas Vanderou Street, the location of one of our featured tavernas, Tzívas, a little way up on the left. Continue on the seafront only a short distance now, then cross the road, walk up Andréa Metaxá for just two blocks, and turn right into pedestrianised **Lithóstroto**.

Stand by for some serious shopping. Elegant, colourful

Fisherman at Argostóli

Lithóstroto is the place to be seen, and where the locals like to relax in the pavement cafés. This was the first stone-paved street on the island, as its name suggests; it's now marble-tiled, and you glide along easily. The **belltower** (8) on the left was built by the

Venetians in the 18th century and now houses a small café run to help those with mental health problems back into employment. Tables are set out in the small square opposite. From here you enter the world of boutiques promoting the latest fashions, brightly lit gold and silver jewellery shops, fancy goods, kiosks for your instant needs, the **post office** (9) and the occasional souvenir shop. The first church encountered on the left is the Roman Catholic church of **St Nikólaos** (10) and a little further along, on the right, is the church of **Ag Spirídon** (11), Corfu's patron saint. There is a good **internet shop** (12) just down the side street before the church on the right, and on the left, in the arcade alongside Metropolis Café is

Venetian belltower on Lithóstroto

Bookmark (13), an English bookshop where you can buy or exchange books.

Looking diagonally left at the end of Lithóstroto, you can see the Archaeological Museum (14) just across the road and, further left, just beyond the traffic lights, the **theatre** (15). Turn left and head up the street on the left of the theatre for just one block: across the road to the left is the **Folklore Museum** (16), just beside the **Korgialenos Library** (17). The museum holds a significant collection of historical items, household bric-a-brac, and costumes, giving a fairly comprehensive picture of life on the island in its heyday. There is also a collection of photographs showing pre-earthquake Kefaloniá.

Return from here back down to the **Archaeological Museum** (14): it's well organised and exhibits vases, tools, sculptures and other artefacts from the Palaeolithic to the Roman period. One whole room is devoted to the Mycenaean period which is an important part of Kefaloniá's early history (see page 104).

Continue down the street by the side of the museum and just opposite Lithóstroto. This leads past the **prefecture** (18) and the **town hall** (19) before reaching the spacious main square surrounded by cafés and restaurants. This is **Platía Valliánou**, named after the national benefactor Panayís Valliános whose statue stands in the square. The square has a great atmosphere in the evening, when the streets around are closed to traffic and alive with diners and strollers. Even with all the dining tables spread onto the square, there is still plenty of room for children to play safely in the centre.

Continue out of the square opposite to where you entered, along **Rizospastón**. The first restaurant on the left, Captain's Table, is popular, but the one we feature, **Arkondikó** (20), is next to it and opposite the **school of music** (21). Rizospastón is a wide street lined with palms and oleanders and full of elegant houses. From here you can cut down right, back to the sea front, not far from where you parked.

St George's Castle

Standing 7 km southeast of Argostóli in a commanding position on top of a peak at an altitude of 320 m, St George's Castle is firmly woven into the history of the island. A survivor of many earthquakes, it stands now in remarkably good condition, and the extensive interior is well worth wandering around.

There are references to the castle as early as the 11th century, but it appears more positively in the history books in 1500, when the Turks had to defend the castle from an attack by combined Venetian and Spanish forces. In 1504 the castle was fortified to its present form, when it became the capital of the island; it remained so until 1757, when Argostóli took on the role.

Arkondikó

A great find for some authentic Greek cooking, and with the right touch of sophistication to feel a bit 'special'. A cosy atmosphere, table mats on polished wood tables, lovely thick napkins and very refined wine glasses. It's on oleander-lined Leofóros Rizospastón, which is pedestrianised at night during the season.

TAVERNA ARKONDIKÓ
Leofóros Rizospastón (close to Platía Valliánou), Argostóli
open all year, but on fewer days in winter
€-€€

large selection of **Greek specialities**, plus **grills** and **fresh fish**.
Sweets and quite a good choice of **drinks** — including a selection of different coffees, cocktails, and even champagne, as well as good **house wine**

Patsoúras

This is another taverna serving consistently good traditional Greek dishes. Frequented by the Greeks themselves — always a reliable guide. Go inside to look at what's on the menu that day to make your choices, but there are also grills and other dishes from which to choose.

restaurants

eat

TAVERNA PATSOÚRAS
Antoni Tritsi, Argostóli
open all year round for
lunch and dinner €-€€

some **specialities**: *kra-sáta xoirinó* (pork in
wine); *loukániko me
piperiá* (sausage with
peppers); *pastítsio*
(baked meat and pasta)
and *keftédes* (meatballs)
served in a tomato sauce

Tzívras

A superb find for Grecophiles in search of a really authentic Greek
taverna, serving some delicious and rarely found Greek dishes.
This is a taverna run mainly for Greeks at lunchtime, which is the
best time to call in for a meal. It may not have an exciting location,
but it is very clean and well run. Look for Tzívras, on the left, not
far along the narrow street heading inland opposite the Shell
petrol station (near the fruit
market on the promenade).

TAVERNA TZIVRAS
Off Ioannou Metaxá, near the Shell
petrol station, Argostóli
open all year at lunchtime and
some evenings €

specialities include *arakás,
fakés* (recipes for both on pages
46-47), *giouvétsi* (recipe on
page 135), *marídes* (small,
whitebait-like fish)

Okra is a popular vegetable in Greece, not usually available in most super markets in the UK — but it can be found in areas with an Asian population. We love this! It goes especially well with chicken and is apparently beneficial in lowering cholestrol levels.

Bámies (Okra)

Soak the okra in vinegar and water for about 15 min, rinse, drain and dry. Cut off the stalk ends carefully to a cone (not as difficult as it sounds — the aim is not to cut off the top, so the seeds remain in the pod).

Heat the oil in a large pan. Soften the onion. Add the garlic, salt and pepper, chopped tomato and okra; cook briefly, stirring gently. Then cover with water and reduce to a simmer. *Do not stir while cooking, or the okra will break up.*

Allow the water to evaporate and just leave the juices, but check the liquid level during cooking. Simmer for about 20-25 min.

<u>Ingredients (for 2 people)</u>
250 g okra
1 tbsp olive oil
100 ml crushed tomatoes or
  1 large fresh skinned and
  finely chopped tomato
1 small onion, finely chopped
1 garlic clove, crushed
salt & black pepper
water to cover

recipes
eat

Kotópoulo lemonáto me patátes (Chicken and lemon with potatoes)

Cut excess fat off the chicken legs, but leave the skin on. Mix the marinade ingedients together. Place the chicken in a container and coat all over with the marinade. Cover and leave in the fridge for a couple of hours or over-night.

Pre-heat the oven to 170°C. To cook, place the chicken legs in a roasting tin with the potatoes. Pour over the marinade and the chicken stock, to almost cover the potatoes. If there is stock left over, save for later in case the liquid requires topping up.

Cover loosely with foil, but remove the foil about half way through the cooking time. Bake for about 1 h 30 min. To keep the chicken moist, baste occsionally.

Serve with a little of the juice spooned over the chicken and vegetables of choice.

Ingredients (for 2 people)
2 chicken legs
2 medium or large potatoes, cut into chunks
250 ml chicken stock

Marinade
50 ml olive oil
50 ml lemon juice
1 level tbsp dried oregano
2 tbsp fresh parsley, finely chopped (retain a little to sprinkle over the finished dish)
2 garlic cloves, crushed
salt & black pepper

RECIPES FROM ARKONDIKÓ

Riganáda

This comes with drinks in the place of the bread basket, a speciality on Kefaloniá.

Drizzle a little olive oil over the toast; add a sprinkling of oregano. Scatter over some tomato and *fetá* cheese. Top with black pepper, a

little more oregano and a scant drizzle of olive oil.

Warm up under the grill or on a barbecue and serve immediately with a sprinkling of balsamic vinegar and chopped fresh parsley.

Ingredients (for 2 people)
2 slices of bread, dampened
    with a little water and
    toasted under the grill or on
    a barbecue
2 tomatoes, finely chopped
25 g *fetá* cheese, crumbled
dried oregano
olive oil
black pepper
balsamic vinegar
parsley (fresh), chopped

Arkondikó saláta (photograph opposite)

Arkondikó's speciality salad is a mix of rocket, shredded lettuce, pieces of cucumber and tomato tossed in a little salt and black pepper and olive oil. Pile on a plate and decorate with pieces of grilled haloúmi cheese, cherry tomatoes and a sprinkling of pine nuts. Quantity depends on the number of servings.

recipes

eat

Be aware that *exohikó (exoticó)* comes in many forms in Greece, this is just one of them. Use boned shoulder or very lean pork belly, which can be rolled, for larger numbers. Increase the stuffing accordingly and adjust the cooking time.

Exohikó (Stuffed belly of pork) *not illustrated*

Pre-heat the oven to 180°C. Mix the stuffing ingredients together.

Place the pork, flat, in a roasting tin, then secure the edges with cocktail sticks or small skewers, leaving a hole in the centre for the stuffing. Place the stuffing in the centre of the pork and press in firmly. (If using one large piece of pork, you may find it easier to lay it flat in the tin, spread the stuffing over, then roll and secure with skewers or string. Slice it before serving.)

Pour over the red wine (if using). Cover loosely with foil initially, but remove this about halfway through the cooking. Roast for about 45 min–1 h (or until the pork is tender).

Serve with mashed potatoes and green vegetables.

Ingredients (for 2 people)

2 x thick lean pieces of pork belly, about 2 cm thick; trim off excess inner fat where possible

50 ml red wine (optional)

Stuffing

25 g *fetá* cheese, crumbled

1/2 pepper (any colour), finely chopped

4 pieces sundried tomato, cut into smaller pieces

Arkondikó saláta

Arakás (Peas)

This is one of our favourite dishes but not widely available in tourist areas. It's good as a shared starter or as part of a meal.

Shell the peas if you are using fresh ones, and cook the peas in some

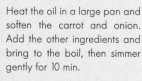

boiling water.

Heat the oil in a large pan and soften the carrot and onion. Add the other ingredients and bring to the boil, then simmer gently for 10 min.

When the carrots are soft, add the peas and simmer for a further 10 min.

<u>Arakás:</u> Ingredients (for 4 people)
500 g frozen peas or 1 kg fresh peas
50 ml olive oil (or 50 g butter)
1 large onion, grated
3 garlic cloves, crushed
1 tin plum tomatoes, drained and chopped, or 3 large tomatoes, skinned & chopped
1 medium carrot, finely sliced
2 tbsp fresh dill weed, finely chopped
salt & black pepper
optional: small pieces of potato can also be added

<u>Fakés:</u> Ingredients (for 2 people)
250 g Puy lentils, rinsed (the no-soak variety)
250 g passata or sieved tomatoes
400 ml stock made with a chicken stock cube
1 small onion, grated
1 garlic clove, crushed
50 ml olive oil
1 bay leaf
salt & black pepper
red wine vinegar to serve (optional)

recipes

eat

Fakés (Lentil soup) *ingredients opposite*

Put everything except the oil and lentils in a large pan. Bring to the boil and add the lentils and olive oil. Simmer until the lentils are soft (about 30 min). Add salt and pepper to taste. Serve with a little red wine vinegar if you like the tang.

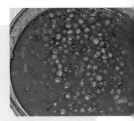

Garídes saganáki (Prawn *saganáki*)

This dish is named for the cooking vessel used in Greece — a *saganáki*. Christos at Stó Psitó (see page 52) suggested adding a little gouda to help bind the ingredients when cooked.

Ingredients (for 2 people)
8 frozen king prawns, peeled and de-veined or 200 g peeled prawns or shrimps
100 ml chopped, skinned tomatoes (1 fresh tomato or tinned)
50 g *féta* cheese, cubed
1 small piece of gouda cheese, grated
1 tbsp olive oil
1 clove garlic, crushed
1 small onion, finely chopped
1 heaped tsp fresh parsley, finely chopped
1 green pepper, thinly sliced
100 ml white wine
salt & black pepper
paprika to taste

Pre-heat the oven to 170°C. Soften the onion, until it's lightly coloured, and the pepper in the olive oil. Add the parsley, garlic, tomatoes and seasoning and mix together (if using fresh tomato, cook a little to soften and reduce the moisture content). Then add the wine.

Reduce the liquid still further, then add the prawns or shrimps. Mix briefly and transfer to a shallow buttered dish. Spread the cubes of *féta* and grated gouda over the top, then some paprika to taste. Bake until the cheese is melted and bubbling (allow 5-15 min — the small shrimps will need less cooking time).

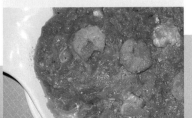

47

A popular walk — especially for visitors staying in Lássi or Argostóli — which follows the old carriageway along the coastline of the peninsula. The walk passes poignant reminders of the massacre of Italian troops during World War Two, but ever-changing views and refreshment options en route make for a delightful stroll.

along the piccolo yiro

WALK

Start the walk along the shore-side road in **Lássi**, by the supermarket next to the access to Gradákia Beach; this is the start of the **Piccolo Yiro**, the old carriageway between Lássi and Argostóli. In around six minutes, you pass a track off left to Kalámia Beach; just beyond it is our featured restaurant, **Stó Psitó** (see page 52). The rural road continues to wend gently downhill past an old estate dating from the Venetian era and along an avenue briefly lined with pine trees. Opposite the point where a descending road joins from the right, is a **pit** where Germans executed 200 officers of the Italian 'Acqui' Division in September 1943.

Distance: 11km/7mi; 3h30min-4h

Grade: easy country lane walk with an ascent of 50m on the return. Take care along the road as it's used by traffic, but there is 1km of footpath.

Equipment: trainers or walking sandals are fine — boots if you prefer

Transport: 🚌 or 🚕 taxi to Gradákia Beach — at the edge of Lássi, before the road rises over the hill to Argostóli

Refreshments en route:
Stó Psitó (at the start)
Katavóthres and Thalassómilos (both about one-third of the way along)
Malstráto (about 1h30min)
Patsoúras (about 1h40min; see pages 40-41)

Points of interest:
Pit and memorial to the massacred Italians
Ag Theódori lighthouse
Ag Theódori church
Katavóthres, a one-time corn mill
Thalassómilos, a sea mill

Ag Theódori Lighthouse is soon reached (**1h**). This was converted from a windmill during the British occupation in 1829 and rebuilt after the 1953 earthquake. It's a pleasant place to sit (see page 55) and enjoy the views and sunsets. Now the road bends right along the other side of the peninsula, passing the small **church of Ag Theódori** on the left, and then **Fanári**

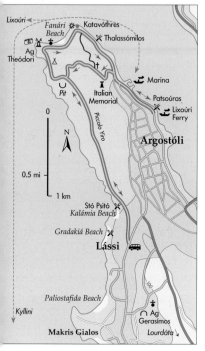

Lixoúri ◄─
Fanári ☀ Katavóthres
Beach
✕ Thalassómilos
Ag
Theódori
⛺
⚓ Marina
Pit
Italian
Memorial
Patsoúras
✕ 🍴
Lixoúri
Ferry
Piccolo Yíro
Argostóli
0
N
0.5 mi
1 km
Stó Psitó ✕
Kalámia Beach
Gradakiá Beach ✕
Lássi 🚌
100
Paliostafida Beach
⛪ Ag
Gerasímos
Kyllini ◄
Makris Gialos
Lourdáta ↓

Beach. Soon you come to **Katavóthres** (see panel opposite). All that remains of the original mill is the water-wheel and water channels. Leave the road now, to walk along the shore-side path shaded by trees. Note a track entering from the right shortly. This leads uphill to the Italian Memorial visited on the return. A little further along the road lies another mill with water-wheel still intact, **Thalassómilos** ('Sea Mill'), once a winery, now an ouzerie/taverna (see page 52).

Continue along the shore until you reach a crossroads (**1h30min**), where the road uphill on the right will be your return route. Turn left downhill here, towards the marina. On the left-hand corner at the bottom is **Ouzerí Malstráto,** where the road bends right towards Argostóli centre. Just continue along the shore now, past the **marina**, until you reach the point from where the **Lixoúri Ferry** departs, a little past **Patsoúras Taverna** on the right (see pages 40-41).

To return, retrace your steps to the crossroads at the

Katavóthres ('Swallow Holes')

There is a curious geological phenomenon at Katavóthres, where sea water pours into a hole in the ground. It pours down with so much force that, back in the 19th century, an Englishman built a watermill to harness the energy.

Where the water disappeared to remained a mystery, until a team of Austrian geologists added 160 kg of a marker dye. They discovered that the water took an easterly subterranean route to emerge partly in Melissána Cave and partly in the springs at Karavómilos on the coast (see page 106).

Following the earthquake, much less water is swallowed now at Katavóthres, and the building there has become the café/ restaurant shown on page 48.

1h30min-point, but keep ahead uphill along the road, which soon bends right as it rises. You will reach the top of the road in well under half an hour. The large **memorial** on the left, where the road bends right, commemorates the massacre in September 1943 of thousands of Italian soldiers of the 'Acqui' Division — an event still remembered each year on the island. Just beyond it, on the right, is a **shrine dedicated to Ag Varvára** (St Barbara, patron saint of the artillery) — a Greek memorial to the tragic events of 1943. Behind the carefully tended shrine, in the woods, are some ruined buildings.

The road begins its descent here. (The track off right, just past the shrine, leads back down to the road after 0.8km and reaches the road just a short way to the right of Katavóthres.) Keep ahead on the road and descend to emerge on the outward route opposite the **pit** (**2h45min**). Turn left here and follow the road back to **Lássi** (**3h30min-4h**).

Stó Psitó

A delightful balcony setting — especially at sunset — above Kalámia Beach. You enter the restaurant across a bridge spanning a pool stocked with fish and striped-necked terrapins. Plenty of choice — from a variety of Kefalonian dishes to some of Christos's own specialities.

With Christos at Stó Psitó; we include recipes for a couple of his specialities.

Thalassómilos

This ouzerí/taverna is in a lovely setting among pine trees, just at the edge of the shore.

STÓ PSITÓ
above Kalámia Beach, Lássi
daily for lunch and dinner in high season, evenings only in shoulder season; there are plans to open weekends in winter €-€€

renowned for their **mezés** — the **tzatzíki** here is delicious!

sweets include mouth-watering walnut cake, cheesecake and tiramisu.

children's menu

THALASSÓMILOS
Thalassómilos, just north of Argostóli
daily for lunch and dinner in season €-€€

extensive menu, ideal for an **oúzo and mezé** break

restaurants

eat

RECIPES FROM STÓ PSITÓ

The versatile dish below can include whatever mix takes your fancy — a great starter for four, or serve as a main vegetable. It can be made the day before, as it is served cold.

Lakaniká Psitá (Roasted vegetables)

Pre-heat the oven to 160°C. Toss all the ingredients, except the balsamic vinegar, in a bowl, then place in a shallow roasting tin. Roast for about 30 min. The vegetables should be softened but not shrivelled.

Place in a dish to cool. To serve, place on individual serving dishes and drizzle over the balsamic vinegar. Decorate with pieces of fresh parsley.

Delicious served with *tzatzíki* (see recipe page 70) and olive oil bread (see recipe page 99).

Ingredients (for 4 people)
3 large mushrooms, quartered
3 peppers, cut into quarters
2 aubergines, cut into large chunks
3 medium or 2 large courgettes, cut into chunks (optional)
2-3 cloves of garlic, finely chopped
1 tbsp olive oil
salt & pepper
sprinkling of dried rosemary and oregano
balsamic vinegar

recipes

eat

Kotópoulo Agriliá (Chicken Agriliá)

In a large pan, soften the peppers in the olive oil, then add the pesto, sun-dried tomatoes, *féta* and olives and heat gently. When the pesto mix is blended, add the chicken pieces and heat through. Add more pesto sauce and olive oil if required.

Meanwhile prepare the rice: heat the olive oil in a pan and soften the pepper, garlic and onion. Then add the rice, pepper, cumin and stock. Cover and simmer gently for 20-30 min (brown rice will require longer). Check the liquid after 15 min and add more water if needed. The rice can of course be plainly cooked in salt water if preferred. For a special occasion, mould the rice in a small bowl and tip onto the plate to serve, as shown here.

Spoon the chicken onto a dish and serve with the rice. Decorate with a whole olive and a scattering of fresh parsley. Can be served with a salad or green vegetables such as peas or broccoli.

Ingredients (for 4 people)

300 g cooked chicken, torn into bite-size pieces
200 g jar of pesto
4 sun-dried tomatoes, or more, cut in half
100 g *féta* cheese
2 peppers, red/yellow, thinly sliced
10 black olives, stoned and cut in half. Save 4 whole stoned olives for decoration.
25 ml olive oil
fresh dill & parsley

Savoury rice

200 g rice — white, wild or brown
500 ml chicken stock (2 stock cubes)
1/2 pepper, finely diced
1 garlic clove, finely chopped
1 small onion, finely chopped
pepper (there is enough salt in the stock cubes)
1 tsp cumin
1 tbsp olive oil

Thalassómilos saláta (Sea Mill salad)

These quantities, for a salad we enjoyed at Thalassómilos, are for four people as a starter; *double* them for a main meal for four.

Place some finely shredded lettuce mixed with some dill and parsley, *lightly* coated with the virgin olive oil and lemon juice dressing, on one large plate or on 4 individual plates.

Arrange the seafood on top. Garnish with cherry tomatoes, cucumber, black olives and parsley. Serve with mayonnaise or *tzatzíki* (recipe page 70) and crusty bread (recipe page 99).

<u>Ingredients (for 4 people)</u>
lettuce, finely shredded
fresh dill and parsley
selection of cooked seafood
   (about 50g per person) —
   shrimps, tinned tuna,
   octopus, crab (or crab
   sticks), smoked salmon (use
   scallops, prawns and mussels
   if octopus isn't available)

Dressing
1 tbsp virgin olive oil and
1 tbsp lemon juice combined,
   with a little pepper

Garnish
cherry tomatoes, cucumber,
   black olives & parsley

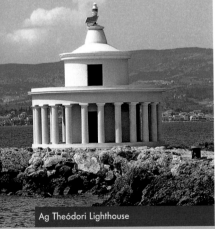

Ag Theódori Lighthouse

Lixoúri is second in size to Argostóli, although it was once the larger of the two and is still a very Greek town; worth wandering around before setting off on this walk to pretty Lépeda Beach. Little remains of the ancient city state of Páli which lies just north of Lixoúri along the coast.

lixoúri and lépeda beach

WALK

The walk starts immediately on leaving the ferry at **Lixoúri**. Turn left along the promenade and soon notice the main square over on the right. This is the place to stop for a coffee and/or have a short wander into the town.

When the promenade comes to an abrupt end, in front of the 'Hellenic Coast Guards' building, walk right and then left, to continue along the road as it bends to the right. Watch the traffic! Soon, turn left along the road signposted 'Lépeda 2km'. Immediately past the **primary school** with the coloured railings on the left and the **police station** across to the right, turn left into the road with a 'P' sign. Soon turn right again and rejoin the promenade, passing Hotel Summery on the right.

Distance: 6km/3.5mi; 1h30min-2h

Grade: easy with a few undulations. The walk is along footpath and a road which ends at Lépeda Beach.

Equipment: sandals or trainers, sunhat, suncream, long-sleeved shirt, long trousers, water

Transport: 🚌 to Argostóli or 🚗 (park) in the car park by the ferry terminal. Then ⛴ ferry from Argostóli to Lixoúri (every half hour, on the hour and half hour in high season, otherwise half past the hour from Argostóli and on the hour from Lixoúri).

Refreshments:
Café Pero in the square at Lixoúri (one of a few places at the start of the walk)
Taverna Apolafsi off to the right about halfway along
taverna above Lépeda Beach (not always open) and a small drinks/snacks cabin on the beach.

You reach the **end of the promenade** (**15-20min**) and leave the town behind. Continue along the road or walk on the grass behind the shore on the left. Away from high season this road is very quiet and peaceful. You pass the cemetery church of

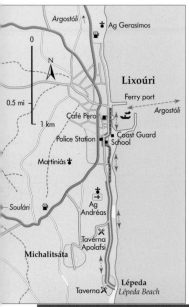

Ag Andréas on the right and then reach some apartments, opposite which is the small beach shown on page 56.

As you rise to a high point, a road goes right to **Taverna Apolafsi**. Keep to the country road along the shore, until you come to a T-junction, with a taverna on the right (not always open). Turn left downhill to **Lépeda Beach** (**45min-1h**). This lovely sandy beach is good for children. There is a shower, changing cubicle, and seasonal snack bar.

Return the same way to **Lixoúri** (**1h30min-2h**).

Café Peros, on the north side of the main square at Lixoúri

Café Peros

Located on the right as you enter the square in Lixoúri (see photograph opposite). Quite popular, especially with older clientèle, and serves a selection of drinks and snacks, etc.

CAFÉ PEROS
main square (north side), Lixoúri
open daily €

freshly squeezed **orange juice** and **speciality coffees** (served either hot or cold) are some of the choices on offer.

Taverna Apolafsi

This family taverna, with its very relaxed ambience, offers a view down to the sea from its elevated terrace. Traditional food cooked by the mother, Tasia.

TAVERNA APOLAFSI
halfway between Lixoúri and Lépeda Beach
open all day €-€€

large choice of **Greek specialities**, like mezé, salads, cockerel in tomato sauce, beef in lemon sauce, grills, fish

restaurants

eat

Biftéki, which translates as 'beefburgers', is often found on menus. These are usually home-made, delicious and hearty, and can be grilled, barbecued or baked in the oven.

Biftéki (Beefburgers)

Mix all the ingredients together for a few minutes. The mixture should bind well but not be too sloppy, so add the egg a little at a time. Divide into four portions and shape into round, flattened patties.

Grill 3-4 min each side, barbecue 5-6 minutes each side, or bake in the oven at 180°C for 20-30 min. The centre should be cooked but still moist.

Ingredients (for 4 large servings):
500 g lean minced beef
1 medium onion, grated
1/2 tsp dried oregano
1/2 tsp dried mint
1 tsp dried parsley (or 2 tbsp of finely chopped fresh)
1 tbsp red wine (optional)
1 thick slice of white bread, dunked in cold water (squeeze out the water and remove the crust)
1 small egg, beaten
salt & black pepper

recipes

eat

Ksifías (Swordfish)

Wash and dry the swordfish steaks and place them in a shallow dish. Mix the marinade ingredients and pour over the fish. Make sure the steaks are well coated. Cover and leave in the fridge for a few hours or at least 30 min.

Heat the grill to medium-high. Drain the fish and grill for 5 min each side at the most. If the steaks are thin, allow less cooking time, or the fish will become dry.

Ingredients (for 2 people)
2 (150 g) swordfish steaks
  (preferably fresh)

Marinade
1 tbsp olive oil
70 ml lemon juice
25 g plain yoghurt
1/4 tsp dried dill or 1/2 tbsp
  fresh dill, chopped
1 tsp dried mint or 1 tbsp
  fresh mint, chopped
1 garlic clove, crushed
salt & black pepper

Lépeda Beach

61

This may seem a short walk, but it will take most of the day to visit the monastery, enjoy a tasting at a nearby winery, and explore old Valsamáta — especially if you round off your outing with a meal at one of the local tavernas. This walk is an ideal way to experience the grape-growing plateau of the Omalá Valley.

ag gerasímos and old valsamáta

WALK

Before starting the walk, explore the monastery complex of **Ag Gerasímos** by ascending the steps and heading along the left-hand side of the imposing new church. The interior decoration is impressive. Apart from Sunday services, the church is mostly open during the summer months. If the church is open, access is through the door along this side. Continue through the old archway at the end into the **convent of New Jerusalem**, founded in the 16th century by Kefaloniá's patron saint (see panel on page 65) The small church here is used during the winter for Sunday services. Leave the church through the imposing bell tower to the left.

Distance: 5.5km/3.5mi: 1h30min-2h, plus time to visit the monastery and explore old Valsamáta

Grade: easy, with a climb of only 30 m from the monastery to the old village of Valsamáta. A walk on a mix of country roads and tracks. *Beware, when exploring the old village, of unstable stonework and hidden holes in the ground.*

Equipment: boots or trainers (not sandals), as the track can be stony in places. Take the usual sun protection and water.

Transport: 🚕 taxi or car to Ag Gerasímos (Ag Yerasímos). Alight or park near the main steps to the new monastery. By car, turn right past the front of the steps, then park.

Refreshments en route: Plátanos Taverna and Koros Taverna in Frangáta

Points of interest: monastery complex of Ag Gerasímos abandoned village of old Valsamáta nearby Robola Winery

Once through the bell tower, **start the walk** by initially going left, then turn right uphill along the **road to Mixáta**. Around 10-15 minutes later, as the road sweeps right, stay ahead uphill on a concrete road. When you meet a cross road/track junction, turn left. The concrete reverts to track almost immediately, as

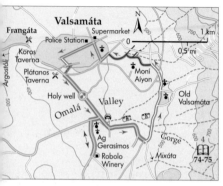

the top of the rise is reached. You walk across a **gorge** which looks like an old gravel pit, and enjoy extensive views down left over the Omalá plain and the monastery.

Soon you reach the first ruins of **old Valsamáta**. The ruin with the pink facade was the barber's shop and possibly also served as a taverna and shop judging by its size. The walls of the **village church (35min)** stand as a monument to the 1953 earthquake which destroyed the village in 50 seconds. Head uphill round the back of the church towards the Venetian-style base of the church tower, and notice the cemetery which is still in use. Further uphill, the old village street continues past a building which might have been used as an olive or wine press. The many ruins along here indicate a once-thriving community. Try not to be too tempted to explore off the main paths/tracks, as these ruins are unsafe and there may be unprotected holes. Exploring this evocative place might take some time so, when you are ready, just return to the church to continue the walk.

Stay ahead along the track past the front of the church and the smaller, more recent **chapel of Ag Paraskeví**. Ignore the concrete road downhill left, which is a shorter route to new Valsamáta (see map). You pass below and to the left of some

Ag Gerasímos

The monastery visited in the Omalá Valley is dedicated to the island's patron saint, St Gerasímos. He was born to a wealthy family in Trikala, Corinthia, and spent twelve years as a young man in the Holy Land.

He settled in Zákynthos on his return, living in a cave at first, before

Ag Gerasímos iconostasis

taking holy orders there. He moved to Kefaloniá and settled in the Omalá Valley, taking over an abandoned chapel to set up a nunnery.

The rest of his life, until he died in 1579, was spent looking after the welfare of the villagers and their children. Many miracles occurred after his death, and when his body was exhumed in 1581, he was found not to have decomposed. He was declared a saint.

ruins that must have been quite an impressive building. Soon you cross a narrow tarmac road. The pleasant narrow track you are on is gradually descending towards new Valsamáta. Where the track dips, about five-six minutes from the church, go downhill on the concrete track to the left. After a few minutes, this becomes a stony track. A high wall on the left marks the boundary of small **Moní Aíyon**. Follow this round to the left and ignore a track joining from the right. Not long afterwards, stay left again, round the bend, as a track joins from the right.

The 1953 earthquake

August 12, 1953: it took just 50 terrifying seconds to reduce the island of Kefaloniá to rubble. The fierce tremor, 7.5 on the Richter scale, ravaged Zákynthos and Kefaloniá, leaving a trail of utter destruction. Every village on Kefaloniá lost public buildings, churches and, worst of all, houses. Every village except Fiskárdo which, for some inexplicable reason, escaped relatively lightly. Some 85% of the island's housing stock was wiped out.

In the face of such devastation to roads and infrastructure, hill villages had to be abandoned in their entirety and reconstruction started again nearer the sea. The first houses built were simple, single-storey buildings, many of which still remain today. It was a decade or more before the wealth and confidence returned to build grander houses. In the face of such hopelessness, many Kefalonians left the island to seek work in America, Australia and New Zealand. It is the wealth of these returning immigrants which gives the island its present prosperity.

Two old, abandoned earthquake villages feature in our walks, old

On reaching a road, turn left (opposite single-storey post-earthquake houses). This is the edge of the **new village of Valsamáta** which lies adjacent to the village of Frangáta on the far side.

When you come to a **major tarmac road** on a corner (**1h05min**), turn right uphill to pass the **church** on the right. Rise to a crossroads with a supermarket across to the right. Turn left here and immediately pass the tiny **police station** on the right. Stay ahead now along this high-level village road until you come to another crossroads, with a **no-entry sign** ahead. Go

Skála and old Valsamáta. Another that you might like to explore is old Fársa. It's above new Fársa, about 12km north of Argostóli. It is perhaps the most evocative of these villages to wander around and can be reached on foot in about 20-30 minutes.

Old Valsamáta — this ruin was the barber's shop.

Park opposite the church in Fársa and start up the narrow, very steep concrete road (also opposite the church). Follow the main route around to the left, and keep to this main track until it reaches a rise, with a telegraph pole to the left and a fire hydrant on the right. At this point take the trail forking uphill to the right and continue all the way up to the ghostly, deserted village — which does, however, have a restored church.

downhill to the left on a narrow concrete road and soon reach another road. Cross this half-left and descend the steps to the main road to Ag Gerasímos. **Plátanos Taverna** is just to the right and **Koros Taverna** a further five minutes to the right.

To return to the start, turn left and just follow the road back to **Ag Gerasímos** (**1h30min-2h**). The **holy well** in the centre of the roundabout is purported to have been dug by Ag Gerasímos himself.

Be sure to fit in a visit to the nearby Robola Winery before heading back to base.

Plátanos Taverna *(photograph opposite)*

A traditional village taverna with an extensive Greek menu. They serve an excellent selection of traditional *mezés* — which can be a mix of many ingredients in small portions — sliced tomato, olives, small pieces of bread topped with *tzatzíki*, two types of village sausage sliced and fried, salami slices, *féta* cheese, boiled egg, cucumber and the like. Like all tavernas, they serve whatever is to hand.

> **PLÁTANOS TAVERNA**
> **main road, Frangáta**
> **open all day in season** €
>
> our particular recommendations would be their **boiled goat, beef in lemon, rabbit** *kokkinistó*, **giouvétsi** **or Kefalonian meat pie**

Koros Taverna

Another traditional taverna situated at the Argostóli end of the main through road. This is the place to sample a superb, home-produced, *robola* white house wine from grapes grown by the owner on his farm. Definitely one of the best white wines we tasted.

> **KOROS TAVERNA**
> **main road, Frangáta**
> **open all day in season**
> €-€€
>
> wide-ranging Greek menu; many **Kelalonian specialities**

restaurants

eat

Stifádo (Meat stew with shallots)

Lamb is the traditional meat for this dish, but beef is more widely used now. Many recipes add the shallots towards the end of cooking, but they are more tender and tastier if added from the start.

Pre-heat the oven to 170°C. Toss the meat in seasoned flour. Heat the oil in a frying pan and brown in the olive oil. Remove to a casserole dish with a slotted spoon.

Add the onions to the pan and lightly brown, then add the garlic, herbs, spices, wine and tomatoes. Bring to the boil, stirring, and pour over the meat in the casserole dish.

Cook for about 2 h, until the meat is tender. Add extra water, if needed, part-way through cooking.

Plátanos Taverna

<u>Ingredients (for 4 people)</u>
750 g lean lamb or stewing
   steak cut into 4 cm cubes
2 tbsp olive oil
1 tbsp flour
300 g shallots, peeled
3 garlic cloves, crushed
400 g tin of chopped
   tomatoes
250 ml red wine (or
   chicken/beef stock)
3 bay leaves
1/2 tsp cinnamon
1/2 tsp nutmeg
salt & black pepper

recipes
eat

Tzatzíki is the ubiquitous accompaniment to most Greek meals. There is often a raised eyebrow if this isn't part of your order but, of course, it's not to everyone's taste. The meat sauce for the *pastítsio* is great with spaghetti — a Greek favourite.

Tzatzíki (Yoghurt dip)
photograph on page 14

Squeeze as much liquid out of the cucumber as possible and mix well with the yoghurt. Add the garlic to taste (you may not want it too strong), a touch of olive oil, a little salt & pepper and dill if used. Garnish with olives to serve. Taste as you go!

Ingredients (for 2 people)
250 g strained yoghurt (see page 29); a medium-thick yoghurt is best, so add a drop of milk if it's too stiff
1 small cucumber, coarsely grated
2-3 garlic cloves, crushed or finely grated
olive oil
salt & pepper
fresh dill, chopped (optional)

Pastítsio (Baked meat and pasta)

Pre-heat the oven to 180°C and start by making the meat sauce. Soften the chopped onion in the olive oil, then add the meat to brown. Keep stirring until the excess liquid evaporates. Stir in the tomato paste, garlic and spice, then the remaining sauce ingredients (if using fresh herbs, add them 10 min before the end of cooking the sauce). Mix well. Leave to simmer gently for 20 min.

Meanwhile, bring a large pan of salted water to the boil and add the pasta. Reduce to a gentle boil for around 15 min, until cooked. Drain and combine with the melted butter, then the egg whites.

While the pasta is cooking, prepare the sauce. Make a roux by melting the butter in a pan. Take off the heat and blend in the flour. Heat gently to cook the flour. Remove from the heat and slowly add the milk (a whisk is useful here). Add the bay leaves, nutmeg, salt & pepper and bring to the boil to thicken, stirring constantly. Cool slightly and quickly beat in the yolks a little at a time. If the sauce is too thick, just add a little milk. It needs to be spreadable but not runny.

Grease a large lasagne-type dish and press half the pasta mix in the base. Add all the meat sauce, then the rest of the pasta. Pour over the béchamel sauce and top with either breadcrumbs or cheese. Bake for about 30 min, until the top is golden brown.

Ingredients (for 6-8 people)
750 g lean minced beef (or turkey)
2 tbsp olive oil
1 medium onion, chopped
2 garlic cloves, crushed
150 ml white/red wine or chicken/beef
  stock
400 g tin chopped tomatoes
40 ml water
2 bay leaves
2 tsp dried parsley or 2 tbsp finely chopped
  fresh parsley
1 tsp dried mint or 1 tbsp finely chopped fresh
  mint
1 tbsp tomato paste
salt & black pepper

For the pasta
250 g penne pasta
2 egg whites, whisked
25 g melted butter

Béchamel sauce
750 ml milk
75 g plain flour
75 g butter
2 egg yolks, beaten with a fork
1/2 tsp nutmeg
2 bay leaves
salt & black pepper to taste

Topping
25 g breadcrumbs or 75 g grated
  hard cheese (*kefalotíri* is ideal if
  you are on the island)

recipes
eat

Most visitors might think Mount Aínos (pronounced Ee-nos) insurmountable, but it is quite a friendly mountain to walk. Even a short foray uphill is easily accomplished, to sample the mountain ambience. Remember that this is a national park, and it is an offence to pick or dig up wild flowers.

mount aínos

WALK

Although Mount Aínos is walker-friendly, it's subject to the vagaries of mountain weather, so be prepared. **Start the walk** at the gate to **Mount Aínos National Park**. Route-finding doesn't need much explanation, as there is a very wide track all the way to the top. Just keep uphill along the main track, ignoring any side-tracks. Amble at your own pace, enjoying the mountain air, flowers in spring and autumn and views which appear through the trees at intervals. A **picnic area**, on the left, is reached at a little over the half-way mark and makes a good spot to rest.

Eventually you will come to a **T-junction just below the summit**. A right turn leads a little further uphill to the very top and the communication masts. Return from this point or turn left and continue along on a fairly level section, for a

Distance: 12.5km/8mi — or 14km/9mi; 5-7h

Grade: moderate-strenuous, with an ascent of just under 600m. But since it's an out-and-back route, you can turn back whenever you like (for example at the picnic area 3.5km along). It takes around 3h at an easy pace (but without stops), to reach the T-junction summit of the walk.

Equipment: hiking boots, water *(at least 1 litre in warm weather)* and the usual sun protection. Early and late in the season take a warm lightweight top plus waterproofs, as cloud can gather around the summit.

Transport: 🚗 taxi or car as far as the gate to the national park (plenty of space to park). If using a taxi, make sure you book your return in advance.

Refreshments: none en route. The nearest tavernas are in Valsamáta (see page 68), Sámi (see page 105) and Karavómilos (see page 76).

Points of interest:
spring and autumn wild flowers
endemic species of fir (*Abies cephalonica*); it was decimated over the millennia by use for ship-building but is now protected
magnificent views through the trees

further 10-15 minutes. You will come to a point where a fork rising to the right leads to an area from where there are extensive views over the southeast corner of the island.

Return the same way to the **park gate (5-7h)**.

Taverna in Karavómilos, with the original water wheel

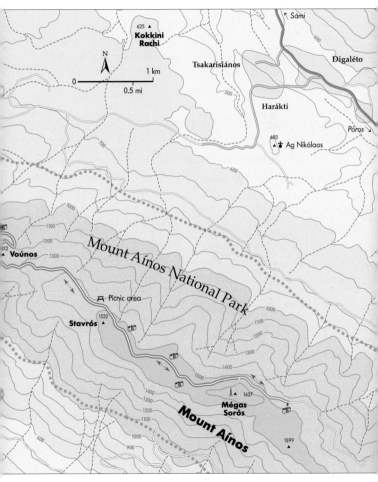

Sámi

625 ▲
**Kokkini
Rachi**

Tsakarisiános

Digaléto

N

0   1 km

0.5 mi

500

Harákti

Póros

700

603
▲‡ **Ag Nikólaos**

600

1000

1100

1200

Voúnos

1300

Mount Aínos National Park

312

⚲ Picnic area

1000

Stavrós 1532
            ▲

1100

1200

1300

1400

1500

**Mégas
Sorós** 1627
        ▲

600

1400

1300

1200

1100

1000

900

Mount Aínos

1599
▲

Karavómilos Taverna

This taverna sits beside the shore of Karavómilos Lake, in company with the original, but now defunct water wheel (see photograph on page 74). The lake is fed by the waters of the Melissána Cave (see panel on page 106). There's a very pleasant outside patio area under tamarisk trees, with views towards Sámi. Plenty of traditional Greek dishes, including fish.

> **KARAVÓMILOS**
> **Karavómilos Lake**
> **daily in season** €-€€
>
> plenty of choice; Greek traditional dishes and fish — perhaps **gópes** (oven-baked small fish); **briam**, a dish similar to ratatouille

Fasolákia (Green beans)

Soften the onion and garlic in the olive oil, then add the tomato, salt and pepper and beans.

Just cover with water and boil gently to cook the beans and reduce the water (this will take approximately 25 min).

Add a drop more water if necessary, but the finished dish should have had all the excess water driven off.

Fasolákia: Ingredients (for 2 people)
250 g runner beans, sliced
1 tbsp olive oil
100 ml chopped tomato, or 1 large tomato, skinned & chopped
1 small onion, finely chopped
1 garlic clove, finely chopped
salt & black pepper

restaurants

eat

Bekrí mezé (Drinkers' appetizer)

Traditionally cubes of pork in wine are used for this dish, served as a *mezé* or as a main course if cooked in a tomato sauce. You can use veal instead. There are many variations of this recipe, but this is our choice as part of a *mezé*.

This recipe needs frequent stirring throughout to stop the ingredients sticking to the pan, as minimal liquid is used in the cooking. Use a good quality meat which tenderises easily. Smaller cubes of meat will need less cooking time.

Heat olive oil in a frying pan. Sauté the onion gently, then add the meat to brown, over a gentle heat, for around 10-15 min, stirring frequently to turn the meat over.

Add the wine and continue to cook gently for a further 15 min, then add the water. Cook a further few minutes, still stirring occasionally, then add the salt and black pepper, allspice and oregano. Stir the ingredients for a further couple of minutes as there should be very little liquid left.

Serve sprinkled with fresh parsley as part of a *mezé* starter.

Ingredients (for 4 people)
300 g pork, cut into 4
  cm cubes
50 ml olive oil
1 onion, chopped
100 ml red or white wine
60 ml water
1 red pepper or pieces of
  red/yellow/green
  peppers, finely sliced
1/2 tsp ground *bakhari*
  (allspice)
1/2 tsp dried oregano
salt & pepper

recipes

eat

An idyllic and atmospheric village, Ássos nestles in a sheltered bay (see also cover photograph) beneath the ramparts of an imposing Venetian castle connected by a thread to the mainland. A great place to unwind, explore the enchanting alleyways and absorb the ambience.

the venetian castle at ássos

WALK

Most visitors toil their way up to the castle along the winding road, but the old footpath we follow has a touch of adventure and romance.

The walk begins in **Ássos** at the start of the road leading to the castle, by the **isthmus car park**. Ignore the first path uphill into the woods on the left, but take the *second* path, just beyond a **fire hydrant**. This rises quite steeply at first, but soon eases out. In around **10-15min**, just past another **fire hydrant** on the right, you meet the curve of a rough track. This service track comes

Distance: 4km/2.5mi; 1h45min

Grade: easy, with an initial short sharp climb, then gradual uphill pull to 120m at the highest point of the walk. The path is slightly exposed on one short section, which may affect those who suffer badly from vertigo.

Equipment: boots or walking shoes, sun protection, water; jumper and waterproof in early/late season

Transport: car or taxi to Ássos. Parking is on the isthmus or the outer loop road.

Refreshments: Tavernas Plátanos and Nirídes at Ássos, but there are other good tavernas as well, according to reports

Points of interest: the castle and Ássos village itself

steeply uphill from the bend in the main track below on your right. Join this track briefly to continue uphill but, almost immediately, rejoin the path on the left.

The path now gently traverses the side of the slope, especially aromatic in spring, with views to an unbelievably turquoise blue sea below. A final curve uphill leads to a back entrance gateway into **Ássos Castle** (**30min**). Stay ahead to reach the main track inside the castle walls.

A left turn here leads to a recently built EU-funded complex still standing empty (it may eventually house a museum). The

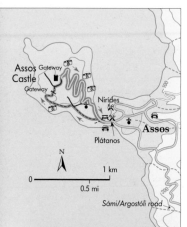

track wanders beyond these buildings.

To head for the main entrance, go right to continue uphill. In more recent times, the castle was used as a prison which worked a thriving agricultural enterprise within the castle walls. It's interesting to wander along trying to imagine what history is contained among the ruins and surrounding foliage. The track leads to the main gateway, built in a dog-leg style which made direct access difficult for invaders.

All that is left to do now is to stroll back down the road, enjoying panoramic views of Ássos along the way, back to the **isthmus car park** (1h45min).

Footpath approach to Ássos Castle

Plátanos Taverna

A delightful taverna in the hub of the village with an amazing menu. A huge variety of Greek dishes from which to choose.

PLÁTANOS
Ássos, daily in season €-€€

the **vegetarian menu** *(diáfora)* includes such mysterious names as 'gypsy food', *stifádo* with rice instead of meat; *anginarokoúkia* (artichokes with peas and aromatic herbs); *gigántes* (giant butter beans); vegetable moussaka, etc.

sweets include a gooey chocolate pudding; *ek mek* (the Turkish name for bread), a honey brioche topped with cream; and *karithópita* (walnut cake with amaretto, recipe page 83).

Plátanos Taverna

NIRÍDES
Ássos, daily in season €-€€

the best bet here is the **fresh fish**, but there are other dishes on offer.

Nirídes Taverna

Nirídes Taverna

Nirídes draws the crowds like a magnet because of its position at the end of the harbour on the seafront.

restaurants

eat

FROM THE MENU AT PLÁTANOS

Pikilía kreá (cold *mezé*) and *pikilía zestí* (hot *mezé*) are both found on many menus on Kefaloniá. They are particularly filling; *one portion is enough for two people* as a light meal. Below is a list of ingredients, and the picture illustrates how they are presented.

Pikilía kreá (cold mezé)

This dish makes an ideal starter or something to have with drinks and nibbles at home.

Hot *mezés* could include fried whitebait, cheese balls (both recipes in *walk & eat Rhodes*), roasted peppers (page 53), courgette balls (page 136), mini meat balls (page 128) and slices of fried sausage.

Ingredients (for 2-4 people)
olives
dolmádes (stuffed vine leaves)
cucumber
tomato
capers
artichokes
spicy cheese dip (page 122)
melitzána saláta (aubergine salad, recipe page 122)
tzatzíki (recipe page 70).

Both versions of the cake on the next page are also found as Kefalonian specialities, although there are a myriad of versions around Greece. The darker walnut version is the one we found mainly, but the basic recipe is the same for both. Use either almonds or walnuts — or a mix of both! I made the almond version, recipe below, and substan-

recipes

eat

tially cut down the sugar content. Greek versions usually have 12 eggs, 12 tbsp sugar, etc.

Amygthalópita or *Karithópita* (Almond or walnut cake)

Pre-heat the oven to 170°C. Grease and line the base of a 21 cm/8 in round spring-form tin or similar.

Separate the egg whites from the yolk. Dissolve the baking powder in the brandy. Whisk the yolks and sugar until creamy, then add the breadcrumbs, almonds/walnuts, water, cinnamon and brandy/baking powder.

Karithópita

Whisk the egg whites and fold into the nut mixture. Pour into the tin. Bake for 20 min or until a skewer inserted in the middle comes out clean.

Leave the cake in the tin and pierce holes all over the surface with the skewer. Pour over the cooled syrup while the cake is still warm, then pour over the optional amaretto. (Some recipes add the finely grated zest of half an orange or lemon — in which case substitute the juice for some of the syrup water.)

When cold, cut into slices and serve with cream or ice cream (but it's equally good served on its own). Will freeze wrapped in foil. Best served the day after it's made.

Ingredients (for 12-16 servings)

150 g ground almonds or walnuts
15 g breadcrumbs
40 g sugar
125 ml water
3 eggs
1/2 tsp cinnamon
1/2 tsp baking powder
12 ml brandy
30 ml amaretto (optional)

Syrup

75 g sugar
1 small cinnamon stick
3 cloves
200 ml water

There are many variations on the **mousakás** theme, but all basically contain the same ingredients. It's a matter of personal taste how you put them together. Some recipes use only aubergines; others (including ours), potato. Anything goes; it depends a great deal on the flavouring.

This is an easy recipe to adjust for any number of people. Even the topping can be a straightforward cheese sauce, béchamel, or one containing egg yolk. We use the béchamel option in this recipe, but it's worth experimenting with the different options.

Frying the aubergines and potatoes can turn this into a very oily (but very tasty) dish. But the aubergine slices can be brushed with oil and baked or dry-fried. Our long-used method is to layer the aubergine (1 cm thick slices) in a dish, drizzling a little oil over each layer: cover with clingfilm and microwave until soft, around 8-10min. Halve the potatoes and boil them until almost cooked.

Mousakás (Moussaka)

Pre-cook the aubergines and potatoes as above. Heat some oil in a frying pan and gently stir-fry the onions and garlic to soften. Add the meat and brown, still stirring. Drain off any excess fat/liquid. Now add the herbs, spices, and salt & pepper to taste. Moisten with the tomato juice if using tinned. Grease a 2.5 l ovenproof dish or large casserole.

Place a layer of aubergine slices in the base of the dish, then the meat. Top with a further layer of aubergine slices and the chopped tomatoes. Finally, place a layer of sliced potatoes on the top.

For the sauce, make a roux with the flour and butter by melting the butter and combining with the flour then, using a balloon whisk, gradually add the milk and seasoning. Continue to stir over the heat until the mixture boils and thickens. (If using a microwave, melt the butter, then add the flour using a balloon whisk to combine the two, and microwave on high for 40 seconds. Gradually whisk in the milk and seasoning. Microwave on high for 2 min, stir, then continue in

1 min bursts, stirring in between, until the sauce bubbles and thickens. Watch carefully, to prevent the mixture boiling over.)

Spread the sauce over the mixture in the dish, sprinkle over some grated cheese and bake at 180° C/gas mark 4 for 30-40 min, until brown on top.

The *mousaká* can be frozen for a few weeks or left overnight on the chiller tray in the fridge, which will enhance the flavour.

Alternative vegetarian version: Replace the meat with about 100 g of cooked puy or green lentils and a mixture of sliced vegetables. For example, heat some olive oil and butter in a frying pan, soften 2 onions, then add 2 sliced carrots, 2 sliced sticks of celery, 4 large chopped tomatoes (or a 400 g tin of tomatoes), a handful of fresh parsley, salt & pepper and an optional dash of red or white wine. Simmer for around 30 min, then add the cooked lentils. Use as the meat layer in the main dish.

Alternative topping: Use the basic sauce recipe, seasoned with salt & pepper, then stir in 1 egg yolk and 60 g of grated cheese.

Ingredients (for 6 people)

500 g lamb or beef, minced
2-3 pre-cooked aubergines (1 kilo)
2 pre-cooked medium potatoes
2 medium onions, chopped
3 garlic cloves, crushed
1 tin (400 g) plum (or chopped) tomatoes, or 4 large ripe tomatoes, skinned & chopped
1 tsp basil
1 tsp oregano
1 tsp allspice
salt & pepper to taste
olive or other oil (to drizzle over the aubergines and for frying)

For the béchamel sauce
600 ml warmed milk
2 tbsp flour
60 g butter
1/2 tsp nutmeg
2 bay leaves
ground black pepper

Picturesque Fiskárdo is at the heart of 'yachtie-land' on the island — it's fascinating to watch the comings and goings in the morning and late afternoon. This is a pleasant walk through tranquil rural countryside, still with signs of a now-lost old way of life. There's also the prospect of a good lunch at Andipáta!

circuit from fiskárdo

WALK

6

Start the walk from the **ferry quay** in **Fiskárdo**: continue along the road by the shore, away from the village. In under five minutes, leave the road and stay ahead on a path, still following the shore. Large **yellow splashes** waymark the route. You reach the cooling shade of pine woods, then the **old Venetian lighthouse** on the right. A minute later, walk to the right of the **new lighthouse** and ignore the path on the right to the shore. Stay with the yellow waymarks as the path forks left; soon you will see ruins ahead. Rise to the **ruined Christian basilica (20min)** and keep ahead through the remains. Ahead is the lighthouse at the tip of the island of Lefkáda.

Once through the ruins, follow **blue dots** and, after descending a stony bank, rejoin the **yellow waymarks**. Very shortly, be ready to fork

Distance: 10.5km/6.6mi; 3h30min

Grade: moderate, with a few uphill sections of around 140m overall. The walk can be split quite easily into three shorter walks:
(1) to Émblissi Beach and back along the road
(2) to Émblissi along the road, then by footpath to Andipáta and Fiskárdo
(3) from Fiskárdo to Andipáta and back

Equipment: hiking boots or walking shoes, sun protection, swimwear, jumper/waterproof in early/late season

Transport: 🚌 or 🚗 car to Fiskárdo. No traffic is allowed in the village, so park along the road to the right on reaching the village or further along in the car park.

Refreshments: plenty of choice, but we feature To Péfko at Andipáta and Captain's Cabin and Lord Falcon in Fiskárdo

Points of interest:
two good beaches
old Venetian lighthouse
early Christian basilica
Andipáta
the abandoned village of Psilithriás
church of Ag Spirídon
Throne of the Queen of Fiskárdo

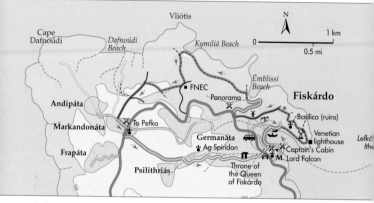

left with the waymarks. In three minutes you rise onto a wide, level strip of land and go right along the central path. The yellow waymarks stop here. Soon you meet a two-wheeled track and follow this to the left. When you come to a **round water storage tank** on the right, a temporary gate barrier may block the way — just go through and replace it. Meet a track a minute or so later and turn left uphill. The track bends right by a **ruined windmill**. Reaching the main road (**45min**), turn right. (Fiskárdo is 0.7km to the left.)

In under two minutes, just before **Panórama Taverna**, turn right down the road to **Émblissi Beach** (**1h**). Go right and continue behind this brilliant white-stone beach; at the far side, pick up the onward path. It's tempting to swim here, but the next beach is even more secluded. Continue by locating the well-defined, stone-edged path leading left off the beach. Turn sharply left uphill in under a minute and rise gently through a forest of strawberry trees and holm oaks on a fairy-tale path.

Fiskárdo harbour

Quite suddenly you arrive at **Kymiliá Beach (1h45min)**, a great place to rest for a while. Then look for the uphill path at the far end of the beach. This soon arrives at a T-junction, where you go left. Gradually climb through woodland for 15 minutes or so and, when you meet a track (**2h**), turn right. The **horse compound** on the left is run by FNEC (Fiskárdo Nautical and Environmental Club), which also runs a sea-rescue team and is responsible for developing paths in the area. Horses are used as transport to check for forest fires and potential problems. FNEC is located in the museum in Fiskárdo and, like all such organisations, depends on public donations.

Just past the compound on the left, go along the stone-lined, **yellow-waymarked** path to the right, signposted to Dafnoúdi. This path rises through woodland. When you come to a stony crossing trail, turn right to dip into a hollow and rise again. Descend a shallow shelf of rock; then, at a crossing trail, turn left uphill (**2h20min**). The path/trail becomes a narrow stone track. Ignore the yellow-waymarked path right to Dafnoúdi, and keep ahead. A minute later, you emerge on the bend of a

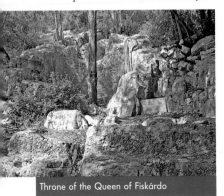

crossing track which goes left. Join this, and stay ahead uphill. In four-five minutes, pass through a barrier gate by '**Anestis House**' on the right and soon meet a road. Turn left to reach **Andipáta** and **To Péfko** taverna (page 92) five-six minutes later (**2h35min**).

Throne of the Queen of Fiskárdo

Leave To Péfko by road, heading away from Fiskárdo, with the **church** on your left. Immediately past the church, turn left on the road signposted in Greek to Psilithriás. This section of road-walking is through pleasant rural countryside. You pass the old village of **Psilithriás** over to the right — mostly abandoned since the earthquake. The old church of **Ag Spirídon** sits in an elevated position, from where Fiskárdo can be seen, but just before it's reached, fork right on a stony track (**2h55min**). In under 20 minutes, as you approach the Kastro Club on the right, the **Throne of the Queen of Fiskárdo** is set back in the trees over to your left. The hollows and steps hewn out of the rock suggest that it might once have been a necropolis. When you reach the main road, cross it and enter the back of **Fiskárdo**; walk past the baker's on the left, to the **harbour** (**3h30min**).

Captain's Cabin

A popular and long-established taverna run by Tassos and his family. Situated right on the waterfront in the middle of yachting activity. Besides good food, you can charge up your mobile phone here and use the internet at Pama Travel, up the steps next door, also owned by Tassos.

Lord Falcon

What an unusual find! A restaurant which serves very good Greek and Thai dishes and is a relative newcomer to the dining scene in Fiskárdo. Not situated on the quayside, but set back from the front with a pleasant garden-style dining area at the back. Good service and a popular venue.

Captain's Cabin (above); Lord Falcon (below left)

CAPTAIN'S CABIN
waterfront, Fiskárdo
open all day in season €-€€

specialities: rabbit *stifádo*, Kefalonian meat pie, Captain's sea food platter (king prawns, swordfish, *kalamári*), vegetarian dishes

LORD FALCON
behind the waterfront, Fiskárdo
open all day in season €-€€€

large choice of Greek, Thai and international dishes

restaurants

eat

To Péfko

A wonderful find, with an interesting menu. The food is delicious and the setting, although by the main road, is side-facing and shaded by an enormous pine tree. The three ladies who run this taverna are constantly experimenting with new ideas (see pages 98-99). The wine's good too!

Their olive oil bread, made fresh twice a day, is absolutely delicious! My efforts at home (see page 99) have gradually worked out, with the addition of some sugar, as Greek flour may naturally contain more sugar. This bread goes well with soup and

To Péfko chefs Arta (left) and Xrisanthe

starters, but it needs to be eaten straight away or frozen. It's a case of experimenting; breads made at home tend to be denser but still tasty.

TO PÉFKO
main road, Andipáta
open all day in season
€-€€

traditional **Greek** and more **unusual dishes**

---

restaurants

eat

Pandzária (Beetroot)

This *mezé* is delicious early in the season, when the leaves are also served with the beets. Warm or cold, it goes well with *skordaliá* (see page 128). Wash thoroughly and cut off the leaves. Boil the beetroot in a large pan of boiling salted water for about 15 min, until tender. Rinse under cold water, then peel while still warm and cut into wedges or slice. Heat the oil in a pan and stir in the leaves until they wilt. Add the cut beetroot, lemon juice and seasoning; mix well.

Ingredients (for 4 people)
1 kg fresh beetroot with leaves
2 tbsp olive oil
1 tbsp fresh lemon juice
salt & pepper

Tonnos (Tuna)

Rub the marinade mix all over the steaks and leave in the fridge for 15 min. Then grill on an oiled griddle or barbecue no more than 2-3 min each side — just to sear (otherwise tuna becomes too dry).

Tonnos: Ingredients
(for 2 people)
2 x 150 g tuna steaks, about
2 cm thick

Marinade
1 tbsp olive oil
1/2 tsp dried oregano
1/2 tsp dried thyme
salt & black pepper

recipes

eat

Kefalonian meat pie is a traditional pie of the island found in almost every taverna, but don't expect them all to be the same — there seem to be almost as many variations as days of the year.

Kefalonítiki kreatópita (Kefalonian meat pie)

Pre-heat the oven to 180°C. Heat the olive oil in a large pan, brown the meat and soften the carrot and onion. Dissolve the tomato paste

in the wine. Add the garlic, wine and tomato paste, parsley, dill and salt and pepper, and mix together well. Remove from the heat.

To prepare the pastry, mix together the flour, salt and sugar. Make a hole in the centre and pour in the oil, white wine, and half the water. Mix together to

Ingredients (for 2-3 people)

500 g lean lamb, cut into dice-size cubes
100 ml olive oil
1 onion, grated
2 garlic cloves, crushed
2 small carrots, finely sliced
1 tbsp tomato paste
150 ml white wine (or water)
20 ml water (added just before cooking the pie)
1/2 tsp ground nutmeg

1 heaped tbsp fresh parsley, finely chopped
1 heaped tbsp fresh dill, finely chopped
salt & black pepper
100 g quick cook rice

Pastry
250 g plain flour
1/2 tsp salt
1/2 tbsp sugar
40 ml olive oil
40 ml white wine

In the past the pie was made from goat, but a mix of meats can be used. Kid doesn't need pre-cooking, but the tougher older goat meat needs tenderising. Beef and lamb seem to be more commonly used now. Some recipes use lentils in place of rice, and some have egg in the pastry. Herbs and spices as well are mainly dictated by personal preference, but parsley is usually found in most pies. Pre-soften the rice a little if it isn't the quick cook variety.

make a pliable dough, adding more water as needed. Knead well together.

Grease a round 20cm/8in cake tin. Line the tin with about two-thirds of the pastry (enough to line the tin and overhang the rim), then roll out the remainder to fit the top of the tin. Place the meat mixture in the tin and scatter the rice over the top to prevent the rice from sinking. Although it may appear to be quite liquid, add the 20 ml of water. Cover the pie with the pastry lid and fold over the edges. Curl the two pieces firmly together and make slits in the centre.

Place the tin in a roasting tin and bake for 1 h, until the crust is golden brown. Leave to settle a short while before serving with peas or perhaps okra.

Fasóli mavromátiko (Black-eyed beans)

Soak the beans in water overnight, then drain. Boil gently in a large pan of water, which generously covers the beans, for about 1 h; add more water if needed. They are ready when they are soft but still firm; do not overcook, or they will become mushy.

Drain and place in a bowl. Mix all the other ingredients with the beans and serve warm or cold. Tasty alone as a vegetable mixed with some black pepper; reheats easily in the microwave.

Ingredients (for 4 people)
200 g black-eyed beans
1 garlic clove, crushed
3 tsp vinegar
25 g olive oil
some chopped fresh parsley
2-3 spring onions, chopped (or 1 red onion, finely sliced)
salt & black pepper

recipes

eat

Spetsofáï (Sausage and peppers in spicy sauce)

The sausage alone makes this quite a spicy dish for most tastes, but for a red-hot version replace one pepper with a hot pepper.

Soften the onions in the olive oil gently, stirring. Stir in all the other

ingredients, except the wine, until well mixed; then add the wine. Cover and cook over a gentle heat for 25-30 min, stirring from time to time.

This is usually served on its own in a clay dish, but for large appetites serve it on a bed of rice or pasta, or with mashed potatoes.

<u>Ingredients (for 4 people)</u>
400 g spicy sausage like pepperoni, sliced
3 large peppers, thickly sliced (usually green, but red or yellow brighten up the dish)
2 onions, sliced
1 aubergine, sliced (optional)
1 400 g tin chopped tomatoes
2 garlic cloves
2-3 tbsp red/white wine or water
2 tbsp olive oil (add more if needed)

Spetsofáï (top) and chicken curry (above)

Kotópoulo me káru (Chicken curry with rice and lemon) (photograph opposite)

Unless you prefer to cook it on the hob, pre-heat the oven to 170°C. Trim excess fat off the chicken legs. In a large pan, soften the onion, then brown the chicken legs. Mix in the garlic, and stir in the tomato paste with the wine. Boil off some of the wine, then add the tomatoes, parsley, cinnamon, nutmeg, salt and pepper. When the chicken is partially cooked, mix 1 tsp of the curry powder with half the lemon juice and pour over the chicken.

Continue cooking gently on the hob or transfer to a casserole; pour over the curry and lemon, and cook 1 h — longer if needed. In either case, baste with the juices occasionally to keep moist.

Bring the 350 ml water to a boil, add the other 1 tsp of curry powder, and boil the rice for 20-25 min (longer for brown rice). Top up the water as necessary.

Place the chicken and some juice on a plate with the rice and pour over the warmed remaining lemon juice. Good with green beans, peas or broccoli.

Ingredients (for 2 people)
2 chicken legs, skinned
60 g soft margarine or butter
100 ml white wine
1 tsp tomato paste
1 small onion, chopped
2 garlic cloves, finely chopped or crushed
2 fresh tomatoes, skinned and chopped or 1 small tin of chopped tomatoes
1 tsp dried parsley or 1 tbsp of chopped fresh parsley
1/2 tsp cinnamon
1/2 tsp nutmeg or ground cloves
2 tsp curry powder (add more for a stronger curry flavour)
75 ml lemon juice (juice of 1 lemon — warm the lemon in a microwave first to increase the juice yield)
100 g rice
350 ml water
salt & black pepper

recipes

eat

TO PÉFKO SPECIALITIES

Kléftiko ('Cooked in a parcel')

Pre-heat the oven to 180°C. Grease two large squares of aluminium foil. Brown the meat cubes in 1 tbsp of the olive oil. Add a further

1 tbsp of olive oil and soften the onion, carrot and potato, stirring. After a couple of minutes add the garlic, peas, oregano and salt and pepper. Cook for a further couple of minutes.

Divide the mixture into two equal portions and place in the middle of the foil sheets. Gather up the sides of the foil a little, to form a bowl. Scatter over the cheese, place tomato slices on the top, and sprinkle over a little more oregano.

Ingredients (for 2 people)

300g lean lamb cut into dice-
  size cubes
2 tbsp olive oil
1 small onion, finely chopped
1 garlic clove, crushed
1 potato, cut into small cubes
1 carrot, thinly sliced
60 g frozen peas
2 tbsp lemon juice
1/2 tsp dried oregano
2 small or 1 medium tomato,
  sliced and cored
50 g *féta* or Lancashire
  cheese, crumbled or cubed
salt & black pepper

Gather in the sides of the foil, to form a sealed parcel and place in a roasting tin. Bake for about an hour. Serve the parcels immediately, on individual plates, with extra vegetables if desired.

Péfko saláta (Pine tree salad)
photograph and ingredients opposite

Toss all the ingredients in a bowl with a little olive oil and the seasoning. Arrange on a plate and drizzle over some balsamic vinegar.

Eleólatho psomí
(Olive oil bread)

Mix the dried yeast and sugar with some of the water to dissolve and activate the yeast, so that it becomes a thin runny paste.

Sift the flour and salt in a bowl and make a well in the centre. Pour in the olive oil and the yeast

paste with most of the water and mix to a soft pliable dough, adding more water as needed. Knead well (about 10 min by hand).

Leave to rise in a warm place for 50 min-1 h (it will double in size). Knead again for a few minutes until smooth. Then divide into roughly 66 g pieces of dough and quickly roll into balls. Place these on a greased and floured baking tray and leave to rise again in a warm place, while you pre-heat the oven to 180°C,

When risen, bake 20-25 min. The bottoms should sound hollow when cooked if tapped.

Pine tree salad: quantities of lettuce and red cabbage have been left to individual taste.

Bread: Ingredients (for 12 rolls)
500 g strong white bread flour
15g dried yeast
85 ml olive oil
1/2 tsp sugar
1/2 tsp salt
250 ml lukewarm water

Pine tree salad: Ingredients (for 2 people)
100 g cooked chicken pieces (bite size)
lettuce, shredded
red cabbage, finely shredded
1 small tin kidney beans, drained and rinsed
1/2 cucumber, cubed
olive oil
salt & black pepper
balsamic vinegar

recipes

Although Sámi is now a modern town and port, it must have been a sight to behold when it was a magnificent walled city, known as Kyatis. It later became an important Roman naval port before its decline. The ancient stones were used in the 13th century to build the Ag Fanéntes monastery, which existed for 600 years.

above sámi

WALK

Start the walk at **Platea Kyprou** in **Sámi**, opposite the **statue to seamen** on the promenade. Head inland along Odós Príamou and soon reach a small **square with a huge plane tree**. Bear slightly left, but stay ahead, to the left of the tree. (A few hundred metres along the road to the left here leads to the remains of Roman baths on the right.) Rise to a T-junction, with a **church** on the left-hand corner, and turn left. In a further minute leave the road, just before reaching a **wall with iron railings**, by turning sharp right uphill on a path marked with a **red dot**. Then turn sharp left uphill a minute later. In another minute, at a **clearing with pine trees** and the remains of some ancient walls, keep left uphill on the main path. A small **retaining wall** jutting out into the path (**20min**) marks the point where the return route emerges from Ag Fanéntes (*turn right here for the shorter walk*).

Stay ahead to continue climbing alongside the valley separating the two hills, initially through woodland. In a few minutes, notice the part-buried remnants of what was possibly

Distance: 5.5km/3.4mi: 2h

Grade: easy-moderate, with a climb of around 280m/924ft, or more if you explore the acropolis hill. A fairly gradual ascent, with a steep descent from Ag Fanéntes. For a shorter walk go directly to Ag Fanéntes from the 20min-point and retrace your steps.

Equipment: hiking boots, water, sun protection, warm top/waterproof in early/late season

Transport: 🚌 (check timetable locally), 🚕 taxi or car to Sámi centre

Refreshments: none en route, but plenty in Sámi including two featured tavernas — Dolphins and O Faros

Points of interest: the two acropolis hills of Ag Fanéntes and Paleókastro (the larger of the two) overlooking Sámi; both were part of ancient Sámi

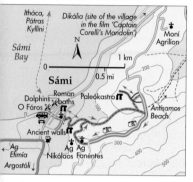

a sarcophagus on the right and another a little further along. When you emerge into the open, you will see the remains of the acropolis on the hill across the valley on the left. The path starts to swing more to the left across the head of the valley. Once at the base of the hill, keep uphill to the right, still following occasional waymarks, to emerge on a flat area.

To continue uphill, bear diagonally left and rise over terraces into a goats' field, with the acropolis of **Paleókastro** over to your left. Keep right along the edge of the field, to the fence and

Captain Correlli's Mandolin

There was a Kefaloniá loved by many before Louis de Bernières' best-selling book, but there is no doubt that both the book and the subsequent film boosted tourism to the island.

Filming the book on Kefaloniá created problems, since the action is set during World War Two, in a pre-earthquake Argostóli. Just a minor hurdle for the film industry — they simply reconstructed a replica of old Argostóli in Sámi and of another village on top of the hill between Sámi and Antísamos.

The locals wanted to preserve the stage set, but the story extends into the earthquake period — so the stage set, like Argostóli, crumbled and collapsed. All that remains now is a noticeboard at the beginning of the track at Dikália showing pictures of the stage set.

road.* To get to the road, climb the bank on the right and skirt round the end of the fence.

Go right on the **road** (under **1h**). (A waymarked path downhill to Antísamos Beach, about 30-40min away, starts just to the left here, then heads right by the goat pens.) You enjoy elevated views of the acropolis walls and then over Sámi harbour. You reach the extensive ruins of **Ag Fanéntes** as the tarmac ends. Keep ahead; the onward route is at the far side of the ruins.

To continue, go down the steps to the left of the bell opposite the entrance to **Ag Nikólaos church** (which is usually locked). This newer church has replaced the

Bell at Ag Nikólaos

*But to explore the acropolis, or as another way to get to the road, stay left along the back edge of the field. Rise gently left onto the next terrace and stay ahead between a huge olive tree down to the right and the hill. When you reach a rough, rising track, follow it to the left uphill to explore further, or go briefly left, then right on a path which leads back to the road. Add 10min/0.6km.)

The Mycenaean cities (1400-1100BC)

There is clear evidence of a well-organised Mycenaean civilisation on both Kefaloniá and Itháca. Major settlements were spread around Kefaloniá at Sámi, Páli, near Lixoúri, Próni, between Skála and Póros, and at Kráni, near Argostóli.

Since the Mycenaeans built with massive stone blocks, remains of their cities are still to be seen. Kráni is one of the best examples, and this is located off the road between Argostóli and Sámi. Just 3.3km after leaving the side of the lagoon, heading towards Sámi, look for the signposted narrow road on the right. It shortly becomes a track, but follow it for 2km to reach the site. Walkways have been cleared around the site, which makes it much easier to get about, and you can explore the very extensive Cyclopean walls shown here.

ruined 17th-century church sited below. Stones line the route of the onward path, but first divert left to locate the steps downhill to the **ruined church of Ag Nikólaos with frescoes**. Then return to the stone-lined path and follow this down the terrace. Stay right initially, below the terrace wall, then head diagonally left down another terrace two minutes later, and again stay right. Head across a bed of pine needles and stay on the path as it winds fairly steeply downhill. Bay trees grow in abundance on the hillside here, so cooks could collect a few leaves to take home on the way down. In 20 minutes or so you meet a crossing path (your outward route); turn left and follow it down to **Sámi** (under **2h**).

Dolphins

A busy taverna located on the seafront road in Sámi, with outside summer dining on the promenade opposite, by the sea. A pleasant place to enjoy a leisurely lunch

> **DOLPHINS**
> Sámi seafront
> open all year, but less often in winter €-€€
>
> **specialities** include a varied choice of Greek dishes; fish (bream and the like); *garídes* (shrimp), *kotópoulo* (chicken)

Above: Dolphins Restaurant (also called 'Delphinia'); below: O Fáros ('the lighthouse')

O Fáros

Another in the row of tavernas with summer dining area along Sámi's promenade overlooking the sea and harbour.

> **O FAROS**
> Sámi seafront
> open all year, but less often in winter €-€€
>
> **large menu** featuring for instance whatever **fish** are in season — *kalamári*, *ksifías* (swordfish); also *mousakás*

restaurants

eat

Melissána and Drogaráti caves

With an island which is virtually a great mass of limestone, it is not surprising to find caves. These two have been organised and commercialised.

Melissána, located not far from Karavómilos, has a collapsed roof and is filled by a lake. A tour of this cave means a 10-minute trip in a rowing boat. An oarsman rows steadily across the lake into a far channel and back again. Legend has it that in ancient times huge stalactites made of pure honeycomb hung in the cave, hence the name (*melissá* means honeybee).

Exploring the Melissána (left) and Drogaráti caves (below)

Drogaráti Cave, south of Sámi and Karavómilos, is visited on foot. More than 100 steps lead down to a platform for the first view of stalactites and stalagmites within an illuminated cavern. Further steps lead down to a walkway circling the lowest cavern which is sometimes used to host concerts. The wet rock and steps can be slippery underfoot, so wear suitable shoes, *not* sandals.

Kalamári tiganitó (Fried squid)

Use fresh or frozen squid. Clean if necessary, then dry thoroughly. The tentacles will be separate, but leave small squid *(kalamárakia)* whole and cut large fish into rings.

All that is needed is to coat the squid with peppered flour and fry in hot fat for about 3 min, until brown and crispy. *Overcooking toughens the flesh.* Drain on kitchen paper. Serve with lemon.

Kolokithákia tiganitá (Battered courgettes)

This dish is great as part of a *mezé* or to serve with drinks. Beat the batter ingredients well, adding enough water to make the batter thick enough to coat the courgettes thinly.

Heat a 2 cm depth of olive/rape seed oil in a frying pan until a drop of batter sizzles. Dip the courgette slices in the batter, shaking off any excess. Fry in the hot oil for a minute, then turn over for a further minute or until golden brown. Remove with a slotted spoon and drain on kitchen paper before serving.

Ingredients (for 4 people)
500 g courgettes, sliced in thin rings

Batter
150 g plain flour
1/2 tsp baking powder
1 tsp vinegar
salt & black pepper
water

recipes

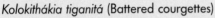

eat

The seas around Kefaloniá are the deepest blue, deeper than we can recall anywhere else in the Mediterranean. It fits Homer's descriptive 'wine-dark sea' so perfectly. This excursion sails across the wine-dark sea to the nearby island of Itháca, legendary home of Homer's great hero, Odysseus.

over the sea to itháca

EXCURSION

Mountainous Itháca (Itháki) is virtually two islands, joined by a narrow neck of land. Píso Aetós, where the ferry docks, lies on this narrow neck, so this car tour first circles the northern part of the island (where there's more to see), then returns south to Vathí.

Follow the road which winds up from **Píso Aetós** to a saddle where the ancient **Mycenaean site of Alalka-menós** is located on the left. It's an open site, so you can wander along marked routes to inspect the giant walls and entrances — but this is best left till the end of the day, when you can fill in time waiting for the return ferry. Within minutes you are descending towards the coast on the far side of the neck and the junction with the main road. Turn left here and head north along the coast road — but not for long, since the road

Description: a full day out, with a 45min ferry ride each way and over 6h to explore Itháca; *see map on page 110*

Transport: ⛴ ferry from Sámi, Póros or Fiskárdo. The Póros ferry is a major line and much more expensive; ferries from Fiskárdo only run in high season. The Sámi ferry is the most regular and reliable: it departs at 08.45; tickets can be bought on the day at the shipping agent on the front, and the crossing takes about 45 minutes. The last ferry back departs at 16.30, which leaves plenty of time for a complete tour of the island (some 70km of driving). There is no point in crossing without a hire car, since the ferry docks on Itháca at Píso Aetós which is about 8km outside the main town of Vathí, and there is no public transport. It's important to mention your intention to ferry across to Itháca when you hire your car, to make sure the insurance covers this option.

Refreshments: There is plenty of choice of tavernas, and most serve the locals, so finding lunch should be no problem. We haven't featured any particular places on this excursion, since it depends on where you happen to be at lunch time.

N
0 ___ 5 km
___ 3 mi

⑥
Fiskárdo

Fríkes
Kióni
Stavrós

Itháca

Anógí

⌖ Moní Katharón

Kefaloniá

⑤
Ássos

*Mírtos
Gulf*

Píso
Aetós

Vathí

Perahóri

Angónas

Ag
Efimía

Kardakáta

Melissáni

Karavómilos ⑦ Sámi

Fársa

Drogaráti

② Lixoúri

Mount Roúdi

Drápano Bridge

③

Argostóli
①
Ag Gerasímos
St George's
Castle

Mount Aínos National Park

④

⑨ Póros

⑧

Ag Gerasímos

Ag
Geórgios

Lourdáta

Skála

Kateliós

⑩

soon leads back over the narrow neck towards the other coast. As you rise away from the coast, take the right turn to Anogí and climb more steeply for a time. Notice, shortly, the road off left to **Moní Katharón**. Dedicated to Panayía Kathariótissa, this monastery is the religious centre of the island. Although devastated by the 1953 earthquake, it was completely rebuilt. The height at this point is 556m, so the views from the monastery — or anywhere on this section of the road, looking down over the highly sculptured and indented coastline around Vathí — are breathtaking.

Stavrós — church of the Sotíras

This high-level route soon leads to **Anogí**, the highest village on the island (520m). Once the island's main town, it's now very sleepy, although there is a café/bar. The eye-catching Venetian campanile is built apart from the church of **Panayía** for protection in the event of another earthquake. The church, with its Byzantine frescoes, is usually locked, but ask in the café and the key holder might be found! The old village lies a little further up the hill.

The descent starts not far beyond here and you are soon down to **Stavrós**. We'd suggest that you keep going, *through* Stavrós and Fríkes to Kióni, then stop to explore these places on the return.

Vathí

Lying in a natural harbour, picturesque **Kióni** is a favoured port of call for holiday yachts, and there is usually a graceful flotilla in the harbour. This settlement developed as the harbour town for the mountain village of Anogí back in the 18th century. A cobbled donkey trail leads between the villages and, although it is becoming overgrown, much of it is still walkable. It starts behind the *kafénion* here in Kióni. **St John's** church, dating from 1790, was also fully repaired after the earthquake. Some traditional houses from the pre-earthquake era are still standing on the left side of the bay.

From Kióni head back to **Fríkes** — another natural and sheltered harbour, also popular with the yacht flotillas. Fishermen from both Exoyí and Stavrós settled here in the 17th century, when piracy was on the decline in the region. Fríkes Bay is a good fishing area, so the fish tavernas are well frequented. Ferries run from here to Lefkáda.

Stavrós is the largest village on the northern part of the island. There is plenty of evidence indicating that this region has been inhabited continuously since the end of the third millennium BC. The relatively recent **church of the Sotíras** (Church of the Saviour) dominates the centre; it was built in 1922 and is unusually austere inside. Opposite is a small park with a bust of Odysseus and a couple of maps, one showing the journey of Odysseus around the Mediterranean and the other tentatively identifying places on the island mentioned by Homer. Looking out from the park there is a view down to Pólis Bay. There are shops in the centre and an archaeological museum with finds from excavations in northern Itháca. This island has its own food speciality, *rovaní*, a rice cake, and it is worth checking the shops here to find it.

Take the main coastal road back now, to explore the southern part of the island. It returns you very quickly down to the neck. Notice the turn off for Píso Aetós, needed for your return to the ferry later, but keep ahead to drive towards Vathí.

Romantics on Homer's trail, wanting to visit the **Cave of the Nymphs**, need to watch out for the right turn just after passing

Dexá Beach. Be warned that there isn't much to see, and the small entrance fee covers the light from the guide's torch — if you can squeeze through the narrow entrance. It's a 2km drive along a very twisting one-lane road.

Vathí is the capital of Itháca and the only town of any significance on the southern part of the island. It lies on the southern shore of the Gulf of Mólos and is surrounded by hills. After the earthquake, houses were rebuilt in the old traditional style. In recognition, it was granted the status of 'Traditional Settlement' in 1982 — which means that all new properties must be built sympathetically. Tavernas line the quayside, so there is a good choice. The square is the hub of the town's social life, surrounded by cafés and bars. There are two museums in the middle of town, the Archaeological Museum (open 08.00-15.00, closed Mondays) and the Maritime and Folklore Museum (open 09.30-15.30, closed Sundays). The Archaeological Museum has a collection of finds, pottery, bronzes and coins, from Alalkamenós and elsewhere on the island. The small island of Lazarétto at the entrance to the port was a place of quarantine from 1668 under the Venetians and English. After union with Greece, it was converted to a jail, but was eventually destroyed by the earthquake.

Perahóri, in the hills behind Vathí, is noted for its wine, but more interesting is the old village of **Paleohóra** nearby. It's full of interesting ruins, including old churches with still-visible frescoes.

From here head back to **Píso Aetós** for the ferry.

Homer's Odyssey

Written in the 8th century BC, Homer's *Iliad* and *Odyssey* are treasured literary epics illuminating so many events in the Mycenaean era. The *Iliad* was based on the last 40 days of the 10-year Trojan War, of which Odysseus was one of the heroes. The Odyssey follows the journey of Odysseus, King of Itháca, on his protracted 10-year-long journey home. Poseidon, God of the Sea, was angry with Odysseus and did everything in his power to prevent him and his companions from returning. Extremely imaginative disasters and adventures befell Odysseus, slowing his return, including being imprisoned for seven years by the nymph Kalypso who took rather a fancy to him. However, Athena, Goddess of Wisdom, finally came to his aid and guided him back to his loving wife, who had spent most of the time beating off would-be suitors.

Odysseus bust in Stavrós Castle

Scholars try relentlessly to identify the places associated with Odysseus, and Itháca and Kefaloniá appear most likely. Both have ancient Mycenaean sites not found on neighbouring islands. Itháca seems to have the strongest claim, but academics are still not wholly convinced and, during our last visit, excavations were in hand on Kefaloniá's Palíki Peninsula to tie that region to Odysseus — arguing that it fits the scenic descriptions more accurately.

Homer's descriptive writing uses some really colourful phrases and his 'wine-dark seas' is one that stays with us and really does evoke the deep purple-blue seas around Kefaloniá.

A walk back in history through the area which was once part of ancient Próni touches on more tangible, recent history in the abandoned village of Asprogérakas. Most of all, you feel the freedom of the outdoors evoked by the ever-changing expansive views almost all the way through this walk.

from ag geórgios to póros port

WALK

8

Start the walk from **Ag Geórgios**: follow the road opposite the pink church, signposted to Kornélos. A café sits on the left corner up some steps. The road becomes a high-level track as the village is left behind. Wander along the hillside absorbing the views on this wide, comfortable corniche track. In 15-20 minutes you pass a winding track uphill right to Kornélos and ancient Próni (called Paleókastro). There is debate as to whether this or the acropolis above Póros (Walk 9) was the most important Mycenaean site.

At the point where the track bends right, there is a **shrine** on the left and **Póros Gorge** lies ahead. Signs of

Distance: 11km/7mi; 3h-3h15min
Grade: easy, mostly downhill, with one short gradual ascent
Equipment: walking boots or trainers, water, sun protection, warm top and waterproof in early/late season
Transport: 🚌 or 🚗 to Póros port, then take a taxi to Ag Geórgios (9.6km). There isn't a taxi rank at the port, but there *is* usually a taxi around and the driver won't be far away. Otherwise, either park and walk over the hill to the taxi rank in Póros (located where the main road enters from Argostóli; 15min) or organise a taxi beforehand for a port pick-up.
Refreshments: none on route, but a café in Ag Geórgios at the start and plenty of choice back at Póros Port and in the town; see pages 120 and 127.
Points of interest:
'ghost' villages of Asprogérakas and Aninata above it
Mycenaean Próni (Paleókastro)

cultivation herald your approach to civilisation, and trees shade the way. Post-earthquake buildings mark your arrival at **Asprogérakas**. Just after a field track goes off right, the corrugated building on the right was once a *kafénion* and shop. At a junction (**50min**) where the track ahead continues to Skála,

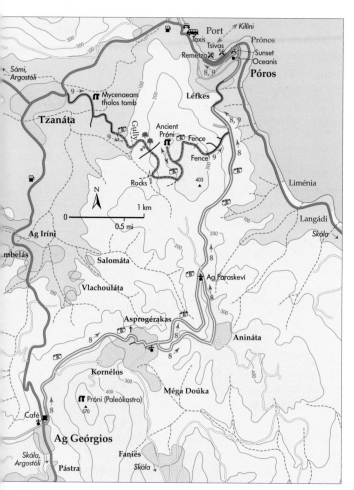

turn left (there is a **well** on the corner here). Then you pass the village **church** — a good spot to sit and reflect. Soon you pass a track uphill right which leads to the other earthquake village of **Anináta**. (The track loops through this village, seen on the skyline ahead, and rejoins our walk at the 1h30min-point, should you want to investigate.) Both Asprogérakas and Anináta were once affluent villages, but became 'ghost' villages after the 1953 earthquake, when many inhabitants emigrated.

Continue along the track round the valley, rising away from Asprogérakas. The Anináta track rejoins from the right at red-roofed **Ag Paraskeví (1h30min)**. Two shaded benches provide an ideal rest stop and chance to enjoy the views. From here the track continues ahead and starts its descent to Póros, with more great views — this time seawards as the track winds downhill alongside the valley on the right. The **gravel crusher** on the left, part way down, was once worked by the villagers. Tarmac and cultivation announce the approach to Póros, and you pass Walk 9 coming in from the left, just before the boundary sign. Póros only developed after the earthquake; it was just a small port at that time.

Soon, when the road forks, keep right. The road reverts to track for a brief section before it bends left in front of the Oceanis Hotel. Turn right here, down the steep concrete road, then go left along the tarmac road to **Sunset Taverna**. This taverna, soon passed on the right, is a great place to stop — or continue down the steps on its right-hand side, to join the main Skála/Póros road. Turn left back to **Póros port (3h-3h15min)**.

Remetzo Café/Bar

An unexpected haven by the sea on the edge of the port area, with a good selection of snacks. Head left, round the far side of the café, to a very pleasant and imaginative bar area among the rocks, set out like the deck of a sailing ship. It's an ideal spot for a light lunch. Sit in comfort and watch the arrival and departure of the ferries and the waves on the shingle.

Remetzo Café/Bar and one of their 'light snacks'!

REMETZO CAFÉ/BAR
Póros port
open daily €

large selection of **drinks**, including our favourite iced chocolate and, of course, cold beer and oúzo

light **snacks** with chips; huge **sandwiches**; various **salad**s, apple pie, cakes and fruit salad

restaurants

eat

Sunset Taverna (Iliovasílema)

This is a wonderful place, especially for an evening meal to watch the sunset, as it sits on the hillside with panoramic views over the port area to Póros beyond. Mum (Niki) produces some delicious food, and daughter Voula acts as waitress, but there is a special treat when things calm down in the kitchen. Voula produces her guitar and sings for the diners — and she's absolutely first class. If she has one of her CDs for sale, don't hesitate to buy one. It has proved one of the best Greek recordings, with full backing, we have brought back from Greece and is professionally produced. An amazing discovery!

> **SUNSET TAVERNA**
> **above Póros port**
> **open daily in season €-€€**
>
> excellent selection of tasty Greek dishes like *pastítsio, giouvétsi, kokkinistó;* fish; grills; stuffed roast pork; walnut cake, *baklavá*

Melizanosaláta (Roasted aubergine salad)

Wrap the aubergines in foil and bake in the oven at 180°C for about 30 min until they are very soft, or microwave, minus foil, for about 10 min. (To get the distinctive smoky flavour of an authentic *melizanosaláta*, the aubergines really need to be cooked on a barbecue.)

Scoop out the flesh and blend until smooth. Add the garlic, salt and pepper, the softened and chopped pepper pieces, then the oil and lemon — slowly, so that the finished mix is firm and not sloppy.

<u>Ingredients (for 4 people)</u>
450 g large aubergines
1 garlic clove, crushed as creamy as
   possible
10 ml olive oil
10 ml lemon juice
salt & pepper
1 small pepper or pieces of different
   colours, briefly softened in the oven
   or microwave, then finely chopped

Tirosaláta (Spicy cheese dip)
not illustrated

Soften the pepper briefly in the oven or microwave, then skin, de-seed and chop into small pieces. Mash the cheese. Put all the ingredients into a blender and whizz briefly. Serve in a bowl as part of a *mezé* selection.

<u>*Tirosaláta* Ingredients (for 4 people)</u>
100g moist *féta* or other soft
   creamy cheese
1 red hot pepper
2 tsps olive oil
1 tsp vinegar

recipes

eat

Kounéli lemonáto (Rabbit in lemon)

Wash and dry the rabbit. Leave to marinate in the wine for a few hours. Remove the rabbit from the marinade, dry and dust with seasoned flour.

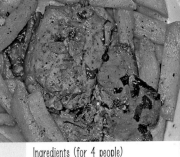

Pre-heat the oven to 180°C. Heat the oil in a pan and brown the rabbit pieces, then place them in a casserole dish.

Stir into the pan the garlic, tomato paste, flour, bay leaves, wine, salt and pepper. (Add a little extra olive oil or water if needed.) Pour this over the rabbit.

Cook for about 1 h 30 min, or until the rabbit is tender. Add the lemon juice about 10 min from the end of cooking. If the juices are still runny, add a little flour paste to thicken when adding the lemon juice.

Ingredients (for 4 people)
1 rabbit, in 4 joints
2 tbsp flour
300 ml white wine
2 tbsp tomato paste
3 tbsp olive oil
5 garlic cloves, crushed
2 bay leaves
1 lemon (juice of)
salt & black pepper

View across the valley towards Tzanáta from the church of Ag Paraskeví

123

Venture inside the vaulted tomb of a Mycenaean king who lived around the time of Homer's *Odyssey*. Then enjoy changing vistas along the valley and climb over the acropolis hill behind Póros. Much evidence of the once-great city state lies scattered nearby, but the views from the top are reward enough for the climb.

the tholos tomb above póros

WALK

Start the walk at **Tzanáta**: follow the signposted track to the **tholos tomb** (**10min**); dating from 1400-1350BC, it is the largest known vaulted tomb in northwestern Greece.

After visiting the tomb, continue along the track for a few minutes, to a **bridge**. Cross the bridge and turn left on a track, following the river on the left. Rise to a gate (which may be open) and continue past a goat-watering place. Swing right uphill, away from the river, on a stony field track (**25min**). This track climbs steeply left uphill, then heads right before levelling out more at the top. Continue round to the left and keep ahead, now with a field on the right. When the route (now a path) forks (**40min**), stay *left* on the well-used path (although the right-hand path was the original route). At this point you are heading in the direction of the Póros Gorge,

See map on page 118

Distance: 6.3km/4mi; 3h

Grade: moderate-strenuous; *only recommended for confident walkers.* Overall ascent of 300m; stony underfoot in places. Numbered signposts and yellow diamond-shaped waymarks are along the route, but are fixed for walkers coming *from* Póros. Look carefully for these if unsure.

Equipment: hiking boots, water, sun protection, warm top/waterproof in early/late season

Transport: 🚌 as for Walk 8 (page 117), but take the taxi 2.8km to the village of Tzanáta and alight just beyond the track off left, on a blind corner, signposted to the tholos tomb.

Refreshments: none on route, but plenty of choice back at Póros Port and in the town; see pages 120, 127.

Points of interest:

Mycenaean tholos tomb (free entry; open until 15.00; closed Mondays) remnants of the ancient acropolis of Próni on top of the hill behind Póros

Mycenaean tholos tomb near Tzanáta

although you cannot see it yet. Start to head more to the right, as the path descends to cross the head of the gully on the left (**55min**).

Keep ahead past a signpost, to reach an area of **plane trees** (**1h**). Walk between a plane tree down left and a **semi-circular stone bench**, then go right uphill, towards **another semi-circular stone bench**, a pleasant spot for a break. Continue uphill to the left of the stone bench, *even where it looks as if branches block the way.* Soon you rise onto a track with a **signpost**; cross straight over and stay uphill on the path. The path winds through holm oaks, heading more to the left of the slope, and at least there is some shade. Don't forget to check for the **yellow diamonds** if you are unsure of the route in places.

When you approach a **rocky barrier** (**1h30min**), you will see a path running ahead through the barrier, but *turn sharp left before the rocks,* to continue uphill and cross back over the stony slope you just climbed. Rise to a **signposted crossing path** and stay left. Nearly at the top, you reach a **signposted path junction**, where you turn sharp right towards Póros. (You could go straight ahead here to seek out remnants of rocks/walls of ancient Próni and return to this point to continue.)

In a minute you rise to the highest point in the walk and first view of Póros through the trees. Descend ahead, to a ledge where the path goes right and downhill. When a **fence** blocks the way (**1h45min**), go uphill to the right, to skirt round the end. Then either continue along this top terrace or, at the first opportunity, drop down to the field below on the left. Stay along the top edge of the field, in the same direction, to meet **another fence** at the end of the field. This blocks the end of a rough track, your onward route, so skirt uphill to the right again, to join the track. Head downhill on this stony track and stay ahead as a track joins from the left. After a steep concreted descent, ignore another track joining from the left. When you meet a tarmac road, turn left and immediately pass the **Póros boundary sign** on the left. Now pick up the **notes for Walk 8** in the last paragraph on page 119, to walk to **Póros port** (**3h**).

Taverna Tsívas *not illustrated*

Less flamboyant than its neighbour, but with much better home-cooked food, the second of two tavérnas uphill from the port in the direction of Skála is our choice down in the port area.

TAVERNA TSIVAS
just above Póros port
open daily in season €-€€

local **Greek dishes** and **fresh fish**; good **house wine**

restaurants

eat

Keftédes (Meatballs)

Mix all the ingredients thoroughly for a few minutes, but add the egg gradually, as the mix needs to be firm not sloppy. Divide into 16 table-tennis size balls and coat lightly with the flour.

Heat 1cm depth olive oil/rape seed oil in a frying pan. Cook the meatballs over a medium heat until they are brown all over and just cooked but moist in the centre.

Drain on kitchen paper and serve with mashed potatoes and a selection of vegetables.

Ingredients (for 4 people)
500 g lean minced beef
1 medium onion, grated
1/2 tsp dried oregano
1/2 tsp dried mint
1 tsp dried parsley (or 2 tbsp of finely chopped fresh)
1 tbsp red wine (optional)
1 thick slice of white bread, dunked in cold water (squeeze out water and remove crust)
1 small egg
salt & black pepper
3 tbsp flour for coating

Skordaliá (Garlic dip) ingredients and photograph opposite

Boil the potatoes in their skins. When cool, discard the skins and mash well. Mash the garlic into a creamy paste and combine thoroughly with the potato. (Taste as you go, as this can be quite strongly flavoured. You may even wand to add more garlic!)

Gradually blend in the olive oil, lemon juice and salt and pepper, until the mixture is creamy but not sloppy.

recipes

eat

Fasolátha (Bean soup)

A Greek favourite which can be made quickly using tinned beans. *If using tinned beans,* heat the oil in a large pan and soften the onion, carrot and celery. Add the garlic and chopped tomatoes, cook a little longer, then add the stock and bring to the boil. Drain and rinse the tinned beans and add to the mixture. Stir and heat again to serve.

If using dried beans, soak overnight in plenty of water. Then strain and put in a pan, well covered with water, bring to the boil and strain. Put the beans in a large pan with all the other ingredients, bring to the boil, cover and simmer for 1 h.

Skordaliá goes well with *tsigaridiá*, Kefalonian 'wild greens' (see page 13).

Skordaliá: Ingredients (for 4 people)
450 g large floury potatoes
4 garlic cloves
50 ml olive oil
1 tbsp lemon juice
salt & pepper

Ingredients (for 2-3 people)
250 g dried white beans (or 2 x 300 g tins of cannelli beans — 360 g drained)
2 small carrots, peeled and thinly diced
1 small onion, chopped
1 garlic clove, crushed
2 small stalks of celery, chopped
200 ml chopped tomatoes
2 tbsp olive oil
600 ml stock (1 chicken stock cube); add more water if needed during cooking

Spread over a large area of hillside, it's difficult now to imagine old Skála being the large and thriving village it was only recently. As you wander around the atmospheric ruins, be aware that they are unstable and best viewed with care. A few properties are being rebuilt by families — for what appears to be holiday letting.

old skála

WALK

The walk starts in **Plátanos Square**, above the shore, at the bottom of the main street through **Skála**.* Head inland, ascending the main street, and stay ahead at crossroads on the edge of the village. After around 15-20 minutes of steady uphill walking, the route levels out. Wandering along this country road, it's difficult to spot the location of the old village on the hillside ahead. The road bends almost parallel with the coast over to your right and passes two **water storage tanks** on the left. Not long afterwards, at a junction, stay left (**30min**).

Distance: 8km/5mi; under 3h

Grade: moderate, with a climb of some 160m — or more, if you clamber around the ruins

Equipment: hiking boots, water, sun protection, warm top/waterproof in early/late season

Transport: 🚌, 🚗 car or taxi to Skála centre (there are parking areas near the shore)

Refreshments: none on route, but plenty of choice in Skála; see page 134.

Points of interest:
Roman villa foundations near Skála
ruins of old Skála

Descend into a dip and, when you come to a track crossing the road diagonally, keep ahead, to start the climb up to old Skála. Ignore tracks right and left, and stay on the road. You pass a track heading downhill to the left (**1h15min**); this is the return route. A couple of bends further on, just after a track joins from the right on the bend, you come to the first ruin in **old**

*Nearby are the foundations of a **Roman villa** with mosaics still intact: to get there, face inland and follow the road left above the shore; it then bends right inland, and the ruins are signposted to the left.

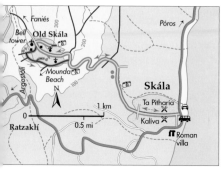

Skála (**1h20min**). The next ruin, on the left, just before the **electricity stanchion**, was the only house in the village with electricity. Further along on the right is an **olive press** with the rusting remains of a diesel engine (made in Bolton by R Fielding). Just before the olive press, on the same side, were the village shops and tavernas and, on the far side, the doctor's house with a *kafénion* next door. The route above leads past ruins of the **school** and **church of the Virgin Mary** then on to Faniés. Follow the next track to the left downhill (opposite where the *kafénion* was located), to the surviving **bell-tower, cemetery** and newly rebuilt **church of Archángelos**, which is accessible. Lower down the hillside is the **spring** and **wash-house**, a mainspring of village life for the women and focal point for village gossip.

Soon turn sharp left, to head back below the village. Watch for a path forking left: this takes you to the **lower spring and wash-house**. (Beware of the roof which was damaged by a boulder during the earthquake.) Return along the same path to the track to continue. A track joining sharply uphill from the right was a major route from the village to Moúnda Beach. After passing an electricity sub-station on the left, look off the track, uphill, for the **ruined church and cemetery of the Virgin Mary**, behind which is another **olive press** and **grape-treading tanks**. Re-join the track.

Soon you meet the road up to the village (the 1h15min-point of the outward walk). Turn right downhill and retrace the outward route back to **Skála** (**under 3h**).

The surviving bell-tower in old Skála

The more traditional tavernas in Skála are tucked away down side streets, but these are the places to go for Greek fare.

Ta Pitharía

A pleasant taverna tucked along a street off right heading uphill off the main village street, just before the large white 'Kinotiki Grapheo' (Council Office) building. Some amusing cartoons adorn the walls, the food is good, and there is a relaxing atmosphere. A well presented appetiser comes with the bread, and a pleasant touch is hot towels with the bill.

> **TA PITHARIA**
> **Skála**
> **open daily in season** €-€€
>
> menu includes varied **soups**; **tuna** with boiled beans, **mousakás** in a clay bowl (with an unusual hint of vanilla in the sauce which works well), **boiled vegetables** excellent **baklavá** with ice cream

Kalíva *not illustrated*

Also sited along a side street on the opposite side of the main street from Ta Pitharia, opposite Greekstones Rent-a-car. An even more traditional Greek taverna atmosphere with an extensive choice of Greek dishes.

> **KALÍVA**
> **Skála**
> **open daily in season** €-€€
>
> hot or cold **pikilía mezés**, **giouvétsi, skordaliá (aliátha)** and **horta**
> **children's menu**

restaurants

eat

Giouvétsi (Youvétsi) (Beef and *manéstra*)

This is a popular dish made with beef and the rice-like pasta, *manéstra* (see page 11).

Pre-heat the oven to 180°C. Dust the meat lightly with the flour and brown in some of the hot olive oil. Place in a large casserole.

Add the rest of the olive oil to the pan and soften the onions. Stir in the tomato paste, crushed tomatoes, oregano, cumin, salt and pepper, and the water. Heat and place with the meat in the casserole. Cook in the oven for 1 h.

Then add the *manéstra*, and top up with water if necessary to prevent the contents drying out as the pasta absorbs the liquid. Check the liquid level at times during cooking.

Cook a further 50 min to 1 h — or until the meat is tender and the pasta soft.

This dish is served in individual clay bowls in Greece — with a selection of green vegetables or a mixed salad.

Ingredients (for 4 people)

750 g beef or lamb, cut in 2.5 cm cubes

300 g *manéstra* (I mainly use *métrio* — medium).

2 onions, chopped

2 garlic cloves, crushed

1 tbsp tomato paste

1 400 g tin crushed tomatoes

500 ml beef or lamb stock (chicken is fine, use 1 stock cube)

1 tsp dried oregano

1 tsp cumin

3 tbsp olive oil

1 tbsp flour for coating the meat

salt & black pepper

recipes

eat

Kolokithokeftédes (Courgette balls)

Grate the courgettes and squeeze out as much liquid as possible. Add all the other ingredients, except the flour, and mix well. Bind together with enough olive oil so that the mixture holds firmly together. Then form

into table-tennis size balls and lightly coat the balls in the seasoned flour.

Heat a 2 cm depth of oil in a pan and fry the balls, turning to make sure they are evenly cooked, for about 6 min. Drain on kitchen paper and serve as a starter or part of a mezé.

Ingredients (for 2-3 people)
500 g courgettes
1 medium onion, grated
100 g hard cheese — *kefalotiri,
graviera* or cheddar, grated
30 g breadcrumbs
70 g plain flour
50 ml olive oil (or enough to
bind)
1 tsp dried parsley or 1 tbsp
fresh, finely chopped
1 tsp dried dill or 1 tbsp fresh,
finely chopped
salt & black pepper
1 tbsp seasoned flour.

recipes

eat

The name of the dish below derives from the pot *'stámna'* in which it's cooked. Originally the lid was sealed with a flour paste, and the pot was buried in the hot ash from a fire to cook.

Stamnáki

Pre-heat the oven to 180°C. Heat the olive oil in a large pan and soften the onion. Stir in the garlic, spices and black pepper, then add the meat coated in seasoned flour to the pan and brown.

Stir in the wine, the stock cubes (dissolved in the water) and the tomatoes. Bring to the boil and transfer to a casserole dish.

Cook in the oven for 1 h, then add the potatoes and carrots. Add the green beans to the casserole in a further 20 min.

Allow 2 h overall cooking time — or until the meat is tender and the vegetables cooked, adding extra water if needed.

Sprinkle over the cheese and leave in the oven a little longer to melt. Then divide into individual serving bowls and serve.

Ingredients (for 2 people)
500 g beef or lamb (not a
    cheap cut), cut into 2.5 cm
    chunks
50 ml olive oil
1 onion, chopped
3 garlic cloves, crushed
1 400 g tin chopped tomatoes
2 large potatoes, cut into pieces
2 carrots, thickly sliced
110 g green beans, sliced
2 beef stock cubes
200 ml water
160 ml red or white wine
1 pinch of ground cloves
black pepper (salt is in the
    stock cubes and the cheese)
1 tsp paprika
2 tbsp flour
50 g *fetá* or crumbly
    Lancashire cheese for the
    topping

Not many people visiting Greece on a casual basis find the Greek language easy to get to grips with. The first obstacle is the Greek alphabet itself. It uses a fair number of characters not represented in the Latin alphabet. In many situations, particularly with place names, road signs and even menus, it is deemed important to change the Greek over to the Latin alphabet to make the names more understandable to foreigners. Unfortunately, there is no definitive or official way to change Greek letters to their Latin equivalent for some of the reasons outlined below. This itself just adds to the confusion, as you will see.

Learning one or two of the pitfalls shown here should help with reading menus in tavernas and with some pronunciations.

The trouble with 'g': On the face of it, this seems a fairly straightforward transliteration. The problem is that 'g' is pronounced as 'y' when preceding 'i' or 'e', but as 'g' in other instances. So a word like *gemistá* (meaning 'stuffed', as in tomatoes or peppers}, is often written as *yemistá* — the way it is pronounced. *Ágios*, meaning 'saint', is another common word regularly mispronounced by visitors. Again the 'g' has a 'y' sound, so it sounds like *áyios*.

The trouble with 'mp': Since the letter 'b' is pronounced as a 'v', it leaves the alphabet without a 'b' sound. To overcome this, a combination of letters, 'mp' is used. This combination is pronounced as 'b' at the start of a word, but as 'mb' anywhere else in the word. The Greek word *mpampou* is a classic illustration. That is how it might be written as a conversion from the Greek alphabet — or equally, it could be written *bambou*. From here it is only a small step to recognise it as 'bamboo'. The mp/mb confusion is commonly noticed on the menu with

GREEK

lamb chops, often seen as 'lamp' chops — which raises a smile with visitors (… but the Greeks would pronounce it as 'lamb' anyway).

'Lamp' cutlets

The trouble with 'nt': This is another combination of letters which is pronounced as a normal 'd' at the beginning of a word and 'nd' elsewhere. It crops up in words like *ntomátes* (tomatoes), which can also appear as *domátes*. This combination is used when a hard 'd' is required, because the 'd' in the Greek alphabet is pronounced as a soft 'd', almost like a 'th'. The word for two, *deo*, for example, is pronounced *theo*.

There are one or two other letter combinations with special pronunciations, but those above are the ones most commonly encountered and the most useful ones to learn.

In the menu and shopping listings, we have used the transliteration that points the way towards the correct pronunciation, but remember that the stress (´) is important too!

CONVERSION TABLES

Weights		Volume		Oven temperatures		
10 g	1/2 oz	15 ml	1 tbsp			gas
25 g	1 oz	55 ml	2 fl oz	°C	°F	mark
50 g	2 oz	75 ml	3 fl oz	140°C	275°F	1
110 g	4 oz	150 ml	1/4 pt	150°C	300°F	2
200 g	7 oz	275 ml	1/2 pt	170°C	325°F	3
350 g	12 oz	570 ml	1 pt	180°C	350°F	4
450 g	1 lb	1 l	1-3/4 pt	190°C	375°F	5
700 g	1 lb 8 oz	1.5 l	2-1/2 pt	200°C	400°F	6
900 g	2 lb			220°C	425°F	7
1.35 g	3 lb			230°C	430°F	8
				240°C	475°F	9

MENU ITEMS

akinós sea urchin

aláti salt

angoúri cucumber

arakás peas

arní lamb

  kokkinistó in tomoto sauce

  kléftiko in filo parcel with veg/cheese

  lemonáto in herb sauce with lemon

brizóles chops

psitó roast

áspro white

áspro krasí white wine

astakós lobster

atherina small, whitebait-like fish

bakaliáros cod

baklavá filo pastry, nuts soaked in syrup

bámies okra, ladies fingers

barboúni fish similar to red mullet

biftékia mince done as a beefburger

bira beer

bouzákia grilled lamb or goat

briám similar to ratatouille

brizóla chop

deípno dinner

dolmádes vine leaves, rolled and stuffed with mince and rice

domátes tomatoes

  yemistés stuffed with rice, herbs and maybe mince

elaiólado olive oil

eliés olives

Ellinikós kafés Greek coffee (never with milk)

  glykós sweet

  métrios medium sweet

  skétos plain, simple (no sugar)

fasolákia green beans

fáva yellow pea purée

féta feta cheese

saganáki sto foúrno oven-baked feta with tomatoes and peppers

filéto filet

fráoules strawberries

fréska froúta fresh fruit

galaktoboúreko filo/custard sweet

galopoúla turkey

galéos cod

  me skordaliá with garlic dip

garídes prawns (pronounced garithes)

g(y)emistá stuffed

g(y)iaoúrti yoghurt

  me méli with honey

g(y)ígantes giant butter beans in sauce

giouvétsi veal in a clay pot with manéstra

glyka dessert ('sweet')

g(y)úros meat from large skewer

haloúmi cheese

halvás sesame/sugar sweet

hoirinó pork

hoiriní brizóla pork chop

horiátiki saláta Greek salad

hortofágos vegetarian

hoúmous hummus

imám baíldi stuffed aubergine

kafés coffee

  frappé iced

me gála with milk

kakáo hot chocolate

kakaviá fish soup

kalamári squid

karidía walnuts

karpoúzi watermelon

kataífi pastry, like shredded wheat strands, soaked in syrup

katálogos menu

krasión wine list

katsíki goat

kávouras boiled crab

kimá mince

keftédes fried meatballs

kléftiko see *arní kléftiko*

kolokithákia courgettes

tiganitá fried

kolokithokeftédes fried courgette balls

kokkinistó veal in tomato sauce

kokteil cocktail

kondosoúvli spiced port on a spit

koniák cognac

kotolétes cutlets

kotópoulo chicken
koukiá broad beans
kounéli rabbit
krasí wine
  áspro or *lefkó* white
  kókkino red
  rozé rosé
krokétes croquettes
kserotígana (thiples) deep-friend pastry
ksifías swordfish
ksúdi vinegar (pronounced kseethi)
ládi oil
lákano cabbage
loukániko sausage
loukoumádes honey-soaked batter balls
makarónia spaghetti
  me kimá bolognaise ('with mince')
manéstra rice-like pasta
manitária mushrooms
marídes small fish (like whitebait)
maroúli lettuce
melekoúni see *pastéli*
méli honey
melitzána aubergine
melitzánosaláta aubergine dip
mesimerianó lunch
mezédes starters (*mezés* for short)

míla apples
moskári beef or veal
mousakás moussaka
múdia mussels
neró water
nes instant coffee
oktapódi octopus
omeléta omelette
orektiká first course, starters
oúzo aniseed spirit
pagákia ice (cubes)
pagotó ice cream
païdákia lamb chops
papoutsákia half aubergines stuffed with mince, tomato & onions, with a cheese topping
pásta cake, pastry
pastéli sesame and honey bars
pastítsio baked meat and pasta dish
patátes potatoes (often synonymous with chips in tavernas)
  tiganités chips (full description)
patzária beetroot cooked with its leaves
pepóni melon
pipéri pepper
piperiés peppers
  yemistés stuffed

with rice and meat
pita pita bread
pítsa pizza
portokáli oranges
proinó breakfast
psári fish
psarotavérna fish taverna
psetó roast
psomí bread
retsína resinated wine
revíthia chickpeas
revíthokeftédes fried chickpea balls
rígani oregano
rúzi rice (pronounced reezee)
rúzogalo rice pudding
saganáki fried cheese starter
saláta salad
saligária snails
  yiáxni in a casserole with tomato sauce
sándouitz sandwich
sardéles sardines
seftaliá home-made sausage
sikóti liver
sikotariá fried liver and kidney
skordaliá garlic/mashed potato dip
skórdo garlic
soúpa soup
soutzoukákia spicy

meat rolls
souvláki meat on skewer
spanakópita spinach pie in filo
spetzofáï sausage and peppers in spicy sauce
stafúlia grapes
ste soúvla spit roast
stifádo meat stew with shallots
sto foúrno baked in the oven
strídia oysters
talagoútes small thick (sweet) pancakes
taramosaláta fish roe paste dip
thalasiná seafood
tiganitá/és/ó (all variations mean 'fried')
tirí cheese
tirokeftédes cheese balls
tirópita cheese pie
tirosaláta spicy cheese dip
tónnos tuna
tost toast
tsáï tea
tzatzíki yoghurt, garlic, cucumber dip
vradinó evening meal
vrastó boiled
yaoúrti yoghurt

141

yemistá/és/ó (all variations mean 'stuffed')

youvétsi veal stew with *manéstra*

zambon ham

zákari sugar

zesté sokoláta hot chocolate

SHOPPING TERMS
general

bottle *boukáli*

kilo *kiló*

half-kilo *misó kiló*

carrier bag *sakoúla*

allspice *bakári* (whole or ground)

apples *méla*

apricot *veríkoko*

aubergine *melitzána*

bananas *banánes*

basil *vasilikós*

bay leaf *dáfne*

beans, french *fasolákia*

beans, broad *koukiá*

beef *moskári*

beer *bíra*

bread *psomí*

bread (olive) *elioté*

butter *voútero*

cabbage *lákano*

cake *pásta*

carrots *karóta*

cheese *tirí*

cherries *kerásia*

chestnut *kastaniá*

chicken *kotópoulo*

chickpeas *revíthia*

chocolate *kakáo*

chop *brizóla*

cinnamon *kanéla*

coffee *kafé*

  instant *nes*

courgettes *kolokithákia*

cream *kréma*

cucumber *angoúri*

cutlets *kotolétes*

dips

  aubergine *melitzá-nosaláta*

  fish roe paste *tara-mosaláta*

  garlic/mashed potato *skordaliá*

  spicy cheese *tiro-saláta*

  yoghurt/garlic/cucumber *tzatzíki*

eggs *avgá*

feta cheese *féta*

filet *filéto*

fish *psári*

  cod, dried *baka-liáros*

  cod, fresh *galéos*

  sword *ksifías*

  tuna *tónnos*

  whitebait-type *marídes*

flour *alévri*

fresh *fréska*

frozen *katepsig-méno*

fruit *froúta*

garlic *skórdo*

grapes *stafélia*

ham *zambón*

honey *méli*

ice

  cubes *pagákia*

  cream *pagotó*

lamb *arní*

lettuce *maroúli*

liver *sikóti*

margarine *margaríni*

meat *kréas*

  on a skewer, for barbecuing *souvláki*

melon (water) *karpoúzi*

melon *pepóni*

milk *gála*

mince *kimás*

mushrooms *manitária*

mussels *múdia*

octopus *oktapódi*

oil *ládi*

  olive *elaiólado*

olives *eliés*

onions *kremédia*

oranges *portokáli*

oregano *rígani*

oysters *strídia*

parsley *maïdanós*

pastry *pastá*

peach *rodákino*

peas *arakás*

pepper *pipéri*

peppers *piperiés*

pork *hoirinó*

potatoes *patátes*

prawns or shrimps *garídes*

rabbit *kounéli*

rice *piláfi*

rosemary *dendro-lívano*

salad *saláta*

salt *aláti*

sardines *sardélles*

sausage *loukániko*

  home-made *seftaliá*

seafood *thalasiná*

snails *saligária*

soup *soúpa*

spaghetti *makarónia*

spinach *spanáki*

squid *kalamária*

sugar *zákari*

strawberries *fráoules*

tea *tsáï*

tomatoes *domátes*

turkey *galopoúla*

veal *moskári*

vinegar *ksúdi* (pronounced *kseethi*)

walnuts *karídes* (pronounced *kareethi*)

water *neró*

wine *krasí*

  white *áspero krasí*

  red *kókkino krasí*

  rosé *rozé krasí*

yoghurt *yiaoúrti*

bold type: photograph; *italic type:* map

INDEX

Second edition © 2009
Published by Sunflower Books
PO Box 36061, London SW7 3WS
www.sunflowerbooks.co.uk

ISBN 978-1-85691-366-9

Cover photograph: Ássos (Walk 5)
Photographs: Brian and Eileen Anderson
Acknowledgements: see page 8
Maps: Sunflower Books, adapted from the latest Road Editions map (see page 27)
Series design: Jocelyn Lucas
Cookery editor: Marina Bayliss
A CIP catalogue record for this book is available from the British Library.
Printed and bound in China: WKT Company Ltd

Before you go ...
log on to
www.sunflowerbooks.co.uk
and click on '**updates**', to see if we have been notified of any changes to the
routes or restaurants.

When you return ...
do let us know if any routes have changed because of road-building, storm
damage or the like. Have any of our restaurants closed — or any new ones
opened *on the route of the walk*? (Not Argostóli restaurants, please; these
books are not intended to be complete restaurant guides!)
Send your comments to mail@sunflowerbooks.co.uk